D0891968

VOLUNTARISM AT THE CROSSROADS

VOLUNTARISM AT THE CROSSROADS

GORDON MANSER

AND

ROSEMARY HIGGINS CASS

 *Family Service Association of America*

NEW YORK

Copyright © 1976 by
Family Service Association of America
44 East 23rd Street, New York, New York 10010

All rights reserved. No part of this book may
be reproduced or transmitted in any form or by
any means, electronic or mechanical, including
photocopying, recording, or by any information
storage and retrieval system, without permission
in writing from the publisher.

International Standard Book Number: 0-87304-140-2

Library of Congress Catalog Card Number: 75-27967

Printed in the United States of America
Designed by Norman Pomerantz

CONTENTS

Acknowledgments 7
Prologue 9
Introduction 11

PART I
A Picture of Voluntarism
1. The Roots of Voluntarism 19
2. The Scope and Extent of Voluntary Effort 39
3. The Volunteer and the Professional 51

PART II
External Forces and Their Impact on Voluntarism
4. The Heavy Hand of Regulation 69
5. Tax Reform 107
6. Back to Advocacy 127
7. The Money Crunch 153

PART III
Structure and Function—Internal Issues Affecting Voluntarism
8. Are Voluntary Organizations Meeting Needs? 183
9. Efficiency and the Economy Mystique 203

Conclusion
10. The Future of Voluntarism 225

Epilogue 247
Appendix: Commentary on the Filer
Commission Report 251
Index 255

ACKNOWLEDGMENTS

IN THE WRITING of any book many persons play a part. We would be truly remiss if we did not acknowledge the invaluable contributions of these "significant others."

First and foremost, we say thank you to those whose advice we sought and who encouraged us in the preparation of the manuscript: to Stanley S. Weithorn, noted tax attorney, for his review and constructive suggestions concerning Chapter 5; to Charles Sampson, Executive Consultant, United Way of America, for historical and other insights on the present and future of voluntary funding; and to Wallace Fulton, Vice-President, Equitable Life Assurance Society, for his wise and witty counsel on voluntarism today.

We also wish to acknowledge our close friends and colleagues during our days with The National Assembly —Elma Cole, John Larberg, C. F. McNeil, Elizabeth Wickenden, and many, many Board members too numerous to name—with whom so much of the material incorporated here was first thrashed out, oftentimes in heated discussions. We particularly appreciate the willingness of Clark W. Blackburn, former Executive Director of Family Service Association of America, to read the original manuscript for us.

Then there was our patient and perceptive editor, Roland Burdick, who knew how to convince us that the changes we did not want to make should *really* be made, and whose calm, dispassionate criticisms greatly enhanced the text. Our appreciation must also go to our research assistant, Yolanda Perotta, who painstakingly found the references we had neglected to note and who checked all our footnotes, and to our typists, Carol Gault and Rachel Burnett, who transcribed our hieroglyphics into English prose so faultlessly.

At home we had the bemused tolerance, but always forthright and wise criticisms of our spouses, Ellen and Peter, without whose patient forbearance we could never have finished the book.

And finally, there are the literally thousands—professionals and volunteers—whose lives have touched our own over the years and whose own efforts on behalf of voluntarism have inspired this book. To them may we say a very heartfelt thank you.

FEW WILL HAVE the greatness to bend history itself, but each of us can work to change a small portion of events, and in the total of those acts will be written the history of this generation.

Each time a man stands for an ideal, or acts to improve the lot of others, or strikes out against injustice, he sends forth a tiny ripple of hope.

And crossing each other from a million different centers of energy and daring, those ripples build a current that can sweep down the mightiest walls of oppression and resistance.

Our future may lie beyond our vision, but it is not completely beyond our control. It is the shaping impulse of America that neither fate, nor nature, nor the irresistible tides of history, but the work of our own hands matched to reason and principle will determine our destiny.

ROBERT F. KENNEDY
*in a speech to students
from South Africa*

INTRODUCTION

VOLUNTARISM is at the heart of the democratic process. A nation which was conceived, born, and went through its tumultuous adolescence by marshalling the strengths of its people in numberless voluntary efforts—from barn raisings to militias to hospitals to symphony orchestras—today is cresting on maturity as it enters its third century. Yet the American democratic experiment faces its most critical challenge today. Just as no country in history has attempted to replicate those political and social processes which our founding fathers established, so no country has succeeded in making completely effective those principles which must undergird political and social processes in a society as vast and complex as ours.

Voluntarism plays a unique role in the democratic process by fostering the widest possible degree of freedom for the individual, through voluntary organizations of his choice, to act, to create, to experiment, to reach out for new goals, and even to fail. But today voluntarism, and hence democracy itself, is at a crossroads and in an agony of transition through which it must pass if we are to realize the universal goals of responsible freedom, equality of opportunity, and respect for the dignity and worth of all individuals.

What, then, is happening to voluntarism and to voluntary effort? What is the era of transition through which voluntarism is passing? And because, almost by definition, a crossroads offers choices of direction, what are the options available to voluntary effort?

We believe there are forces impinging on volunta-

11

rism today which are capable of radically changing its traditional characteristics—diversity, freedom, creativity, flexibility, and advocacy, as well as the extent and character of volunteer participation. In the aggregate, these forces are little understood. One reason is that their impact is neither cataclysmic nor instantaneous. It is not like the business which fails overnight or the product which is suddenly displaced by a new invention. On the contrary, the effects are incremental and cumulative. It becomes important, then, to understand not only what is happening to voluntarism today, but also to place today's events in a historical perspective.

Some of the forces with which we shall deal in this book are affecting voluntarism directly and critically. These forces include what might be called a money crunch, compounded by inflation, changing relationships with government, changing role and status of volunteers, and lack of public understanding. In addition, there are powerful societal forces which also operate to affect the shape of voluntary effort. Among them are the increasing scale of our society—in population, urbanization, and the centralization of power in government, labor, and industry; the increasing acceptance of the concept that all people—young, old, black, white, men and women of every ethnic, racial, and religious background—have a right to participate in decisions affecting them; the increasing interdependence of all persons, nationally and internationally. Further, one sees an eroding of confidence in our major institutions and a questioning of traditional values as they have been applied to work, to the family, and to authority.

In looking at the capacity of the voluntary sector to respond and to adapt to the aggregate impact of these forces, one of its most significant characteristics has been its adaptability. Even more important there has always been a core of motivated and committed leadership (sometimes volunteer and sometimes professional) which has historically responded to the challenge to lift voluntary organizations out of their customary mold, or to create new ones and project them into patterns seen as responsive to emerging needs. We believe that the best leadership of the voluntary field is ready and waiting to do this. A choice of direction tomorrow will be helped by an enlightened perspective on where voluntarism finds itself today.

This, then, is why this book "has to be written." We feel a measure of responsibility to share our concerns, our insights, and our experiences with a wider audience, in the hope that they will be useful to those upon whom the responsibility for leadership rests. That the vital spark of voluntarism should be allowed to flicker or to be extinguished seems unthinkable, and yet there is disquieting evidence that this is precisely what is happening. When an officer of a major foundation said recently that the impact of current forces is resulting in "death by erosion" he was talking about foundations, but he might well have been uttering a profound warning for the entire voluntary sector in the present critical period.

The Bicentennial period would seem a doubly appropriate time to assess the condition of voluntarism. Indeed, a candid appraisal of voluntarism should be an integral part of any evaluation of the American Revolution and the meaning and purpose of the American experience over the past two hundred years. It is our hope that it will aid in an understanding which we think necessary if present trends are to be reversed, if traditional values are to be reaffirmed, and if a sense of commitment is to be regained. Only through such a process can each of us contribute to making voluntarism a revitalized instrument of individual fulfillment and institutional achievement for the public good.

As coauthors, we speak from different, but complementary vantage points. One of us has served for a number of years as a volunteer in a variety of health and welfare organizations, at the local, state, national, and international levels; the other has served as a professional in social welfare throughout his career, similarly in local, state and national organizations. Both of us have been very active in professional associations, one the bar, the other, social work, and the perspectives of each have been widened by significant volunteer experience in local and national structures of our churches, in organizations seeking to advance the arts, and in neighborhood groups. Thus our varied experiences have taken us into related areas of voluntary effort. One of us speaks for the volunteer and is concerned with the sum of volunteer effort and the future of volunteerism; the other has had more experience in the instrumental forms which voluntarism takes. Together, these two elements, the volunteer and the organization, make up voluntarism as we use it in this book.

We define voluntarism as:

Those activities of individuals and agencies arising out of a spontaneous, private (as contrasted with governmental) effort to promote or advance some aspect of the common good, as this good is perceived by the persons participating in it.

The essential element is responsible freedom: freedom to act in accordance with one's own will or choice, not from constraint, and independent of the government. These elements and concepts become important as one later examines the current scene.

In addition to definition we must also draw some parameters around the scope of the book. Voluntarism, as we shall see later, encompasses a vast universe of action, effort, and organizations, both formal and informal. Indeed, the more formal field of voluntarism encompasses such widely diverse activities as health, the arts, the environment, professions and unions, social welfare, education, the sciences, and religion. We speak, however, out of backgrounds which have been predominantly in the fields of health, social welfare, religion, and law, the areas of which we have the greatest knowledge. But many of the forces, problems, and issues with which we deal are pervasive of the entire field of voluntarism and it is hoped that our discussion may be useful across the broad spectrum of voluntary efforts of all types. One of the subjects about which we have strong conviction is the commonality of many problems for all of the voluntary sector, and the necessity for the sector to stand together in these areas of concern.

In a real sense this book is dedicated to those volunteers who serve as board members, as committee members, or who deliver services of one kind or another, and without whose commitment and efforts the entire voluntary enterprise would collapse overnight. We hope it will have more than a passing interest to the professionals who live daily with the effects of the kinds of problems which we will consider, and who, in partnership with the volunteer, must make their unique contributions to find solutions for survival.

As we conclude this Introduction the reader may be aware of our conviction, or perhaps bias, on this subject. Indeed, we believe deeply in voluntarism and in the best of the traditional values which it represents; in the intrinsic capacity of voluntarism today to offer individuals an opportunity to participate in projects for the community good and to exercise a forceful voice in decisions affecting their own lives; in the ability of voluntary effort and action to contribute to the solution of societal problems; and in voluntarism as a primary force which can make our democratic society function more effectively, in terms of choice among long-range goals, and with a view toward improvement of the quality of life for all.

PART I

A PICTURE OF VOLUNTARISM

Measured by the active goodwill, efforts, time, and talents of millions of persons and by its impact on society over the sweep of history, voluntary effort represents the unfolding of humanity's highest and noblest impulses.

1 ROOTS OF VOLUNTARISM

ONE MUST SEARCH far back in the history of western man for the origins of voluntary effort. From the very beginnings of human experience, as modern sociology and anthropology have evidenced, man has striven to share with as well as to destroy his fellowman. Starting with the family, the kin, and extending to the tribe and the early communities, men and women had to cooperate just to survive in the face of hostile environments, as well as of hostile strangers.

Over time efforts to "promote or advance some aspect of the common good" have taken two forms, either individual or associational. As we shall see, the pages of western history recount numberless instances of individual effort to promote the common good—frequently at great sacrifice or even risk. The impulse for these acts is to be found in the Judeo-Christian ethos of love, justice, and mercy. The millions of volunteers of every type in our society today can trace their lineage and inspiration to these devoted efforts.

Although people have banded together since the beginnings of time for many reasons, modern associational forms of voluntary effort were stimulated by the Reformation and its accompanying movement toward freedom of association, flowered with the urbanization of society during the industrial revolution, and experienced their greatest expansion during the twentieth century. These organizations exist to fulfill an incredible variety of purposes, ranging from the individual needs of their members to services to individuals and to communities. While voluntarism encompasses all types of voluntary groups our principal concern in this book will be with those institutions which are organized to serve others, in contrast to those which primarily serve the interests and needs of members.

The history of voluntary organizations which in some way or other serve others illuminates two rather contrary approaches to the solution of problems of human need which have existed down to the present day, perplexing the greatest minds of all ages. One view emanating from the Greek and Roman experience sought social reform as the answer to the social problems of the community. Another view, principally derived from the early Judeo-Christian heritage, believed that there was little one could do to overcome or change the particular social status in which one found oneself. One sought to alleviate the sufferings of one's fellow human beings as they passed through this "vale of tears," confident with Saint Paul that "the sufferings of this life were not worthy to be compared to the glory of the next." Thus, while the concept of mutual aid is as old as mankind itself, its evolution took two divergent paths, one very ancient which was only revived in the seventeenth and eighteenth centuries and the other which had its flowering in medieval times and is still of tremendous significance in voluntary effort today, but inadequate of itself. What is evident today is that both individual service and social reform are necessary if we are to solve the myriad social problems with which we find ourselves confronted.

In looking briefly at the chronicle of voluntary effort one is struck by the extent to which it has contributed to the development and shaping of governmental services, and conversely, the extent to which governmental services have in turn tended to shape the direction of voluntary effort. Thus, passing reference to some of the more significant public developments provides a frame of reference for better understanding of the role of voluntary effort. Similarly, the role of organized religion as a source of education, social welfare, health, and other services has been of crucial importance throughout history even as today. At no time was this more important than during the Middle Ages when the church was virtually the only organized force which perpetuated the Judeo-Christian ethic through tangible acts of service and mercy.

While Greek democracy was far removed in practice from our concept of democracy—excluding women, slaves, and the foreign-born from citizenship—some of its most renowned thinkers, such as Solon and Cleisthenes, sought both privately and through legislation to institute social reforms designed to lift up the poorer citizens and remove some of the burdens they bore. However, charity and philanthropy were not conspicuous virtues among the early Greeks, and Aristotle was constrained to commend foreign examples of benevolence in his *Politics,* the while he endeavored to point out that, unless the purposes of civil and social life were carefully considered by those seeking to effect change, no amount of individual or associated action would be sufficient.

Similar to the Grecian was the Roman attitude toward the needs of the disadvantaged. While the sufferings of the poor stirred the consciences of few of the wealthy Romans there were some with power who sought social reform. Tiberius Gracchus and his brother, Caius, were instrumental in the achievement of land reform—for which they sacrificed their lives. Tiberius had witnessed the starvation and idleness of the Roman citizens while wealthy men of the province of Tuscany profited by the labor of slaves on their vast land holdings. Curiously, the *lex frumentaria* of Caius, which gave Roman citizens the right to purchase grain from the public stores at about half price, began the demoralization of the Roman plebians. This system continued until the greater part of the Roman populace was enabled to live in idleness, dependent on what came to be a free distribution of grain at the public charge. No one of the emperors dared to change this system because the Roman citizen was a voter and would support whoever gave him bread and circuses. Perhaps, if the warnings of Aristotle had been known and listened to, the strengths of the Roman empire would not have been dissipated and other social reforms leading to more humane conditions for all would have been introduced. Or, had Seneca, the Roman philosopher who saw man's obligation to do good to everyone, been listened to, again the course of history might have been different.[1]

What did appear on the scene and saved western civilization from disappearing entirely when the Germanic hordes began to besiege the Empire was a new philosophy of life which, in its purest form, embodied the highest concept of assistance to others. This was Christianity whose founder had said, "This is my commandment, that you love one another as I have loved you. Greater love than this no one has, that one lay down his life for his friends." (John 15:12–15)

Christianity had its roots in Judaism and stemmed from a tradition of help which had developed over hundreds of years. Among the Jewish people the duty of kindness to the poor, to the widows and to the fatherless was constantly shown to be pleasing to God. More than this, their notion of justice included all ethical conduct. The word for charity in Hebrew is *Sedakah* or righteousness. Nowhere is the whole concept better expressed than in the oft-quoted words of Micah, "What doth the Lord require of thee, but to do justice and to love mercy and to walk humbly with thy God." (Micah 6)[2]

Many of the precepts of the Jewish tradition are spelled out in the Old Testament, particularly in the Book of Deuteronomy where Moses says, in Chapter 14, 28–29, for example:

> At the end of every three years you shall bring forth all the tithe of your produce in the same year, and lay it up within your towns; and the Levite, because he has no portion or inheritance with you, and the sojourner, the fatherless, and the widow, who are within your towns, shall come and eat and be filled . . .

The stories of Ruth and Naomi and the help extended to them by Boaz, and of Tobias who daily went about helping the afflicted are typical illustrations of the charity which inspired many of the ancient Jews, the same charity which enabled them to endure and to assist one another through centuries, first of domination by other nations and later of bitterest Christian persecution.

The eight degrees of charity defined by Maimonides in the Middle Ages spell out further the purpose and dignity of the Jewish concept of charity. Lowest on the scale is charity given meagerly and by a person as if forced; somewhat higher is charity contributed adequately but only after it is asked for; even better is aid given in such a manner that neither the giver nor the person assisted knows the identity of the other; and highest of all is assistance that enables a person to achieve self-support by helping him to find work or to open a business. Thus the concept of social justice has always been at the very core of Jewish values. On three things the world rests, the rabbis have said: (1) the study of the Torah—the body of religious precepts and teachings, (2) prayers, and (3) acts of loving-kindness, embracing not only gifts of funds but also personal service. It is this same charity that has succeeded today in building a vast network of the finest humanitarian services ever known to exist.

One of the dominant aspects of the Christian message was its universality. No one was exempted—neither rich nor poor, man nor woman, the known sinner, the feared and often despised foreigner, the freeman nor the slave. The idea of a spiritual freedom which made all people brothers and sisters, the promise of another life of true happiness, the notion of sharing with one another—these revolutionary concepts were greatly appealing not just to the poor and the disenfranchised, but gradually to the wealthy and powerful, who began to accept and then themselves to promote the new message.[3]

The early Christian communities endeavored to provide help to the poor, the sick, and the afflicted. A little later came the monasteries, at first built far from the cities and thus removed from the people and then gradually, between the fifth and the ninth centuries, coming to serve as oases of learning and help to those in need.[4] In these centuries, when the conversion of a tribal leader or king meant the conversion of all his people, the knowledge and the practice of Jesus' message of love of one another was not easily achieved. Neither warring lords, eager to consolidate their power, nor poverty stricken peasantry struggling just to survive against the physical elements had time or inclination to do other than ignore the beggars who were everywhere, and cast out the most unfortunately ill —the lepers, those who had the plague, and the mentally ill. On the other side, church leaders, missionaries, bishops, and priests waged a continual struggle, reminding all of their common brotherhood, of their duty to share with one another, to love as Christ had loved.

With the advent of Charlemagne and the birth of the Holy Roman Empire in the year 800 there began a somewhat uneasy marriage of church and state which endured for the next five centuries and brought extremes of greatness and of depravity. This era saw in the Cluniac reform a vast expansion of monasteries which were seats both of learning and of social services of every kind, and, in the spirit of St. Francis of Assisi, the beginnings of lay movements to help the poor, the sick and the old. On the other hand the Crusades, which had ostensibly been initiated to free the Holy Land from the hands of the Mohammedans, became at the hands of many unscrupulous warriors the occasion for plunder, rape, and the persecution and killing of Jews and Mohammedans. Paradoxically the same Crusades were responsible for the development of many kinds of voluntary assistance which have existed down to modern times. Though antedating the Crusades, the hospices in Jerusalem for the pilgrim and the sick spread to western Europe and groups of men, religiously inspired, formed what became known as groups of hospitaliers. At the same time the privations of captivity came to the fore during this epoch and several religious orders were founded to help and to free the captive.[5] Meanwhile, at home the feudal system provided a type of rudimentary welfare in that the lord or the count considered himself responsible to provide not only protection for his people but also, in exchange for their labor, assistance in time of illness or famine.

In the aftermath of the Crusades came the great Bubonic Plague of the early fourteenth century. Already, cities had begun to wield dominant influence, to create new social and political patterns, and to reflect new associational forms. The older agrarian economy was beginning to yield to one dominated by trade and commercial enterprise, cities had begun to win their freedom from bishops and princes, and a new class of free citizens developed. Interestingly, the medieval guilds which were found in all these cities and which provided aid to members and their families were probably the first to assess their members for a type of insurance premium so as to provide for the widows and children of prematurely deceased guild members.

The plague decimated Europe's population and within a few years of its eruption was taking the life of one out of every three persons. There was no cure for it and so the ministrations of the countless religiously inspired served only to alleviate the pain of the dying and to bring spiritual comfort. The bravery of persons like Johannes Tauler in France, Catherine of Siena in Italy, Philipp Nicolai in Germany, Valerius Herberger in Poland, to name but a few, served as both example and inspiration to their fellowman.

Throughout medieval history there is little, if any, emphasis on social reform. Charity is commanded by Jesus but as interpreted it is charity to the individual. The results of the Reformation, cataclysmic in so many ways, were to affect as well the multitude of these charitable endeavors which had become part and parcel of the western experience. Foremost among these activities had been aid to the poor, which all over Europe took the form of almsgiving. Gradually the monasteries had been partially replaced by "hospitals" *(hôtels Dieu)* which ministered to the old, the sick, pregnant women, and abandoned children. But many were left to wander the countryside and it was these to whom the Church had said it was charity to give. Meanwhile, local and state governments sought to contend with the beggars, many of whom were able-bodied, and as far back as the time of Charlemagne, a statute was enacted forbidding the giving of alms to those who could be self-sustaining.

The struggle was exacerbated by the Reformation. Luther appealed to the princes of Germany to forbid begging and instead to organize in each parish a "common chest" out of which food, clothing, and money could be distributed to the needy. Similar plans for relief were set up in Switzerland, France, Austria, and Scandinavia. In this same period the forerunners of the modern social worker, the Daughters of Charity, were founded in France by St. Vincent de Paul to devote themselves to charitable work, especially that of nursing the poor.[6]

Meanwhile in England, where all of the monasteries and convents had been secularized by Henry VIII and their properties confiscated by the state, it became necessary to devise some new method for the care of the poor, who had formerly been cared for voluntarily by groups within the Church. A series of enactments in the sixteenth century by the English Parliament culminated in the adoption of a codification known as the Poor Law of 1601. Responsibility for the poor, now recognized as governmental, rested with the local community, the parish, but was limited to persons who had been born there or had been resident for three years. Funds were provided by a general tax. Three classes of poor were distinguished: (1) the able-bodied poor who were sent to workhouses or, if they refused to work, to jails, (2) the impotent poor, those who were unable to work and who were either sent to almshouses to live or, if it were less expensive to maintain them in their homes, given food, clothing, and fuel, and (3) dependent children, some of whom were placed with any person willing to keep them, or sold to the lowest bidder, or indentured to a townsperson to learn a trade, the boys until they were twenty-four years of age and the girls until they reached their twenty-first year or were married.

With some modifications these laws prevailed in England until well into the nineteenth century, when in the wave of the Industrial Revolution various social reform movements for better health, better working conditions, and housing and prison reform culminated in a number of pieces of legislation making more humane the conditions for all of the poor and the disadvantaged. Important too in this era was the creation in London in 1869 of the Society for Organizing Charitable Relief and Repressing Mendicity, shortly to be known as the Charity Organization Society, which coordinated the activities of private and public charities. Its format soon provided a model for similar groups in other cities in Europe and the United States. Operating on the philosophy first put into practice by the Reverend Thomas Chalmers, a Scottish minister, of helping the poor to help themselves, and emphasizing an individualistic approach as well as seeking to find a solution to the cause of the problems of the poor, the Charity Organization Society laid the early foundations for what we today call "casework."[7]

What is noteworthy of the period in history from the Protestant Reformation to the present day is the ever-increasing necessity for the involvement of government in the solution of the problems of health, social welfare, education, housing, and working conditions. Starting with the vacuum precipitated when the Christian Church was displaced in its efforts to care for the needs of the people, fostered by Lutheran teachings about work and the separation of church and state; impelled by the unification of nations; and further carried along by the tumultuous changes in the aftermath of the Industrial Revolution, the scientific advances, and the concomitant population increases—governments, at first most reluctantly, came to recognize the responsibility, which they alone could meet, for providing for their citizenry what the citizens alone could not provide for themselves.

But where is voluntary effort in all of this? Were it not for the crusading efforts of many individuals in the eighteenth and nineteenth centuries, much of the European reform movement, ultimately translated into new private groups and into legislation, would never have eventuated. This was equally true in the United States, where the somewhat feeble beginnings of voluntary effort can be traced to pre-Revolutionary days. Though the Colonies felt Dutch and French influences, it was the English influence which predominated, and many of the now basically governmental patterns familiar at home were incorporated into the early colonial treatment of the poor, the aged, the ill, and the abandoned. In principle, the Colonies adapted the Elizabethan Poor Law, with two major adjustments, to the New World. Where in England the poor were more often assigned to almshouses, in the Colonies it was customary to provide "outdoor relief," that is, relief in kind—food, clothes, and fuel. In England legacies and endowments made possible the support of many poor in hospitals, asylums, and orphanages but such private charity did not exist in the Colonies. However, colonial churches were active in providing help, albeit only to members of their own congregation. A singular exception was Pennsylvania, which so long as it remained under Quaker influence, was an example of humane treatment to all within its boundaries, as was also early Catholic Maryland.

The sad fact remains that there was little of true charity or benevolence in the voluntary or legislated activities of the American colonists in the seventeenth and eighteenth centuries. As Carter has noted,

> . . . Abiding belief in the depravity of the unfortu-
> nate had been imported to the North American
> colonies by the most pious and energetic of the
> early settlers. Everything they found here
> confirmed their outlook. The new land was a
> place of opportunity beyond all precedent, a
> milch cow incapable of running dry. There
> seemed to be no excuse for an American who
> failed to exercise his free, individual initiative in
> acquisition of personal property. In exchange for
> resourceful toil, he could have anything he was
> determined to get, and the God of his fathers, as
> interpreted by Calvinism, or a variant, would
> bless him forever.[8]

The poor tax was therefore resented, the poor were despised and degraded and frequently cruelly treated. Yet it
must be remembered that the life of many of the colonists
was one of great privation. Many lived in remote settle-
ments, in constant fear of the recurrent attacks of the
Indians. Mutual aid was one thing but there was little
place for the unfortunate, especially if it appeared that the
misfortune was of one's own making. Nevertheless, as the
cities along the coast began to flourish, there arose a host
of civic and charitable activities.

In this period the work of Benjamin Franklin
stands out. Inspired by the writings of the famous
preacher, Cotton Mather, Franklin went beyond him in
believing that men should show their gratitude to God "by
the only means in their power, promoting the happiness
of his other children." Among his achievements were the
part he played in the establishment of a free library, the
Pennsylvania Hospital, and the Academy, which later became the University of Pennsylvania. He founded a volun-

teer fire department and developed plans for cleaning and lighting the streets of Philadelphia. He emphasized the importance of self-help but also the need to band together in projects for the general welfare.[9]

The new nation, an experiment in democracy, also found itself an experiment involving a variety of social problems. While its earliest tasks seemed to be to deal with poverty and ill health, others very soon appeared on the scene. There were the blind, the deaf, the mentally deficient, the homeless, the abandoned, the mentally ill. Then, beginning in the 1840s, came wave upon wave of immigrants, most with a language barrier, all with different cultural expectations and perceptions. They needed places in which to live, work, and worship, as well as education to fit into this new society, and many other special services. Ethnic societies, many of them religiously inspired, were set up to help the immigrant to become assimilated. The earliest settlement houses provided a unique service to these sometimes bewildered persons and at the same time awakened the sensibilities of many of the well-to-do to the plight of the poor. A conspicuous example of voluntary effort was provided by the Jewish communities, which provided a wide range of services to meet recognized needs—relief societies, orphan homes, clinics and hospitals, institutions for the aged, and others.

The nineteenth century, which saw the abolition of slavery, the wrenching effect of the Civil War, the rise of industry and the birth of labor unions, saw also the birth of many voluntary social service organizations, the establishment of many private schools and colleges, a vast expansion of health services and hospitals (a number of which had earlier been part of the almshouses), and the initiation of special institutions such as the Perkins Institute for the Blind in Watertown, Massachusetts, the Asylum for the Deaf in Hartford, Connecticut, and the Germantown (Pennsylvania) School for the Mentally Deficient. Similarly, the organization of the United States Sanitary Commission in 1861, financed by private means, to "combat filth and disease" in Union army camps during the Civil War laid the groundwork for organizing state departments of public health.[10] Many of the persons responsible for the establishment of such agencies had borrowed techniques already developed in England and on the Continent. Thus came the first American YMCA in 1851, the efforts at prison reform inspired by the work of John Howard and Elizabeth Frey, and the foundation of the American Red Cross impelled by the work of Jean Henri Dunant, the Swiss banker, to name but a few.

These voluntary groups sprang up for a variety of reasons: reaction to the admittedly inadequate governmental care of the poor, desire to aid special groups in the population, the effective propagandizing of the social reformers, and the desire of many religious groups to provide for the needs of their own within the doctrine and structure of their church. The desire for the exchange of information and a forum to discuss mutual problems led to the organization in 1873 of the National Conference of Charities and Corrections (now the National Conference on Social Welfare) while the Charity Organization Society movement, another offshoot from English tradition, beginning in Buffalo in 1877, represented in part an effort to bring local agencies into closer working relationships. These proved to be the forerunners of the present health and welfare councils and the councils of social agencies.

During the first half of the twentieth century an enormous proliferation of every type of voluntary organization imaginable appeared on the scene—local, regional, and national. To cite but one example from the health field: its concern with education, research, and treatment of specific diseases led in this period to the creation of at least seventy-five national disease-oriented agencies.[12] The country's borders stretched from one ocean to the other and the diversity of its religious and ethnic groups led to the founding of thousands of voluntary groups for every possible interest and need—recreational and sports groups, choral societies, farmers' co-ops, men's service organizations, homes for the aged, professional societies, mental health facilities, youth-serving organizations, and myriad others.

But the efforts of voluntary organizations and local and state governments to cope with the problems of the poor, the unemployed, the aged, and the chronically ill became increasingly inadequate to meet the mounting demands. The federal government, which philosophically had up to this point denied its responsibility in these areas, was forced by the Great Depression of the early 1930s to a complete reversal of its thinking and an acceptance not only of its obligation to provide for relief of economic distress but also of the right of needy persons to assistance without a loss of respect for their dignity and worth as human beings.[13] Various forms of emergency relief were enacted, and the first permanent Social Security legislation was passed in 1935. Amendments to the legislation in intervening years have extended coverage to greater numbers of persons and the institution of Medicare in the 1960s has provided a renewed sense of security for the growing percentage of older persons for whom the cost of health care has reached astronomical proportions.

President Johnson's "Antipoverty Program" of the 1960s saw the inauguration of many innovative programs which involved persons at the local level in solving, with governmental and nongovernmental funds, and, through governmental and nongovernmental agencies, some of the persistent problems that have been, over the generations, afflicting American life. That this program was not more successful was attributable to a number of complex factors beyond the scope of this limited survey but including such endemic human failings as political machinations, malfeasance, and the failure of too many Americans to look beyond the costs in tax dollars to the ultimate benefit that this would bring to the nation as a whole. The alternative offered, "revenue sharing," has meant the abandonment of many human services programs begun in the sixties.

Ironically, in the depths of the Depression, it was because the many voluntary organizations and local and state governments were inadequate to fund and man the programs needed to sustain the massive numbers of unemployed that the federal government finally took a hand. Today, nearly fifty years later and with a nation twice as large, where resources of voluntary groups are more strained than ever (as we shall see at a later point in this book), and where many a state and city is on the verge of bankruptcy, the federal government is turning back to these agencies and jurisdictions some of the very responsibilities it had assumed. There appears to be a lack of recognition that many problems are national in scope, transcending state and local boundaries. Whether such a policy is justified or realistic at this time must be left to history.

In chapters to come we shall look at the scope and extent of voluntary effort in our nation, and at the roles of volunteers and professionals, then move to a discussion of some of the major forces and constraints impinging on voluntarism, and finally cast an eye on the future of voluntarism, if it is to have a future. For the moment we want to focus on the historical significance of this tremendous force which, in its best expressions, has acted in these last two centuries as a catalyst to unite the two historically divergent approaches to which we referred at the beginning of this chapter: social reform and individualized charity. Our society has fallen heir to a social philosophy rooted in Aristotle and Aquinas, furthered by the writings of Locke and Mills, and given a practical reality in the Constitution and its interpretation by our Founding Fathers and by major decisions of the United States Supreme Court, particularly those of the twentieth century in the area of social jurisprudence. Unwittingly, the religious thinkers of the Protestant Reformation, with their concepts of governmental responsibility, set the stage as well for the reform efforts made during the eighteenth and nineteenth centuries when the Industrial Revolution turned upside down the still predominantly agrarian societies of the western world.

The enlivening principle which has kindled efforts at social reform has been the Judeo-Christian concept of love of one's neighbor. Without it social reform is stunted and cut off at its roots, having only self-interest as its motivating force; and when altruism is no longer apparent, as perhaps in the aftermath of the first exciting days of the Antipoverty Program, it dies. The idea of one common humanity, of the basic dignity and worth of all persons without exception, has been the inspiration for countless legions to give of themselves in service to others.[14]

Yet for many centuries those animated by love of their fellowman did not take the next step to change the social conditions which precipitated poverty or illness or other misfortune. It is the current century which has seen the nexus of individualized charity and efforts at reform. Thus, we will assess in greater depth in chapter

6, the growing new emphasis on voluntary organizations of every kind as spokesmen and prime movers toward change.[15]

This is what voluntarism has given historically to our nation. Now let us look at where it is today.

NOTES

1. For an interesting historical discussion of the early development of charity and philanthropy, cf. EDWARD GRUBB, "Philanthropy," *Encyclopedia of Religion and Ethics,* 9, pp. 837–840.

2. LOUIS FINKELSTEIN, J. ELLIOT ROSS, and WILLIAM ADAMS BROWN, *The Religions of Democracy* (New York: The Devin Adair Company, 1941), pp. 17–18. See also EDWARD GRUBB, op. cit.

3. The development of the social teachings of the Christian churches is extraordinarily illuminated in the work by ERNST TROELTSCH, *The Social Teaching of the Christian Churches,* Vols. I and II, trans. by Olive Wyon (New York: The Macmillan Company, 1931).

4. Ibid., Vol. I, pp. 162–164.

5. HEINZ VONHOFF, *People Who Care, An Illustrated History of Human Compassion* (Philadelphia: Fortress Press, 1971), pp. 44–47.

6. WALTER A. FRIEDLANDER, *Introduction to Social Welfare* (Englewood Cliffs, N.J.: Prentice-Hall, 1968), pp. 10–13.

7. Ibid., pp. 16–37, especially pp. 22–23 and 32–37.

8. RICHARD CARTER, *The Gentle Legions* (New York: Doubleday and Company, Inc., 1961), p. 31.

9. ROBERT H. BREMNER, "Private Philanthropy and Public Needs, Historical Perspective" (unpublished manuscript, Ohio State University, Department of History), pp. 12–13.

10. WALTER H. TRATTNER, *From Poor Law to Welfare State,* (New York: Free Press, 1974), pp. 68–71.

11. GORDON MANSER, "Voluntary Organization for Social Welfare," *Encyclopedia of Social Work,* 15th ed., p. 824.

12. Ibid., p. 825.

13. WALTER A. FRIEDLANDER, op. cit., p. 120

14. Cf. RICHARD M. TITMUSS, *The Gift Relationship: From*

Human Blood to Social Policy (New York: Pantheon Books, 1971).

15. DOUGLASS CATER, "The Keynote Speeches," *Report of the Conference on Voluntarism and America's Future, February 1972* (Washington, D.C.: Center for a Voluntary Society, 1972), pp. 10–11.

2 THE SCOPE AND EXTENT OF VOLUNTARY EFFORT

AMERICANS HAVE LONG been called a nation of joiners. The oft-quoted remark of de Tocqueville early called attention to what he regarded as a peculiarly American phenomenon, and historical and sociological works of the first decades of the twentieth century continued to pay lip service to this platitude. From more recent studies which have sought to analyze the truth of this statement has emerged the finding that membership in voluntary associations is not as characteristic of Americans as once thought[1] nor as unique a phenomenon of American life.[2] But participation in voluntary associations is positively associated with democratic society, with increasing urbanization, and with the openness of the society.[3] Since the United States was the first modern political democracy, perhaps de Tocqueville was more prophet than observer. The fact remains that voluntarism has been a significant force in American life from its very beginnings, with varying effectiveness in its impact, but always a force to be reckoned with.

But before making any assessments, we must ask what we mean by voluntarism, volunteer, voluntary action, philanthropy, and charity. Each of these words conveys as many different connotations as there are readers. For example, to some *voluntary action* means the work of volunteers; to others, it denotes lobbying or legislative action; *philanthropy* carries for many an unfortunate overtone of wealth and privilege (perhaps the avoidance of taxes through charitable gifts), yet this contrasts with the dictionary meaning which defines philanthropy as "the love of mankind, especially as manifested in deeds of practical beneficence."

The word *charity* has had a varied history. Originally it was in favor and general use, then it passed out of favor, and now it once again appears to be coming back into wider usage. Its origin as a legal term appears in the English Law of Charitable Uses, but it found its way into the U.S. Internal Revenue Code in 1894 when corporations, companies or associations organized and conducted for charitable, religious or educational purposes were declared to be exempt from taxation. Similarly in 1917, very shortly after the enactment of the first personal income tax, the law instituted inclusion of a deduction for individual contributions to "corporations or associations organized and operated exclusively for religious, charitable, scientific or educational purposes . . ." The disfavor into which the word charity fell derived from its association with the "Lady Bountiful" notion of "doing something for the poor." (Some years ago one of the authors reviewed the personnel file of an applicant for a social work position who listed as one of her qualifications that she had spent a summer in Europe "browsing among the poor"!)

We will use the words *charity* and *charitable* when speaking in a legal context, especially as related to contributions and tax status. On the other hand, we will use the word *philanthropy* to refer to the broad field of voluntary activity, including health, education, the arts, social welfare, religion, civic and environmental concerns. We shall avoid, however, the use of the phrase *voluntary action* except within the specific context of legislative action and lobbying.

Scholars who have attempted to define voluntary organizations and associations have encountered similar problems of definition. David Horton Smith, who has made significant contributions in this area, classifies organizations into "established" organizations, which are nonprofit and nongovernmental, but basically nonvolunteer, making wide use of paid staff, as contrasted with "volunteer" groups, in which the predominance is of volunteer staff and members. Another way he categorizes them, admittedly imprecisely, is into organizations whose objectives are primarily "self-serving" in terms of the affairs and interests of the members, and those primarily "other-serving" in the sense that their primary goal involves improvement of some aspect of the larger community or society.[4]

Alan Pifer usefully describes three principal types of voluntary groupings.[5] The first is the spontaneous coming together of citizens in support of a cause; the second, local or national organizations devoted to the economic and social interests of participating groups, such as labor unions, trade associations, real estate boards, and Chambers of Commerce; and the third, established service organizations and institutions devoted to the common or general good, such as health, welfare, educational, cultural, artistic, and musical. Pifer's second group roughly corresponds to Smith's category of "self-serving" organizations, and his third group to Smith's "other-serving" groups.

Other categorizations of organizations would include instrumental (primarily concerned with activities beyond the group itself) and consummatory (primarily concerned with existence and activities of the group itself),[6] and established service (again primarily oriented to others) and self-help organizations. Our use of *voluntary organization* (agency) covers both Smith's "established" and "volunteer" groups. Where more specificity is needed, as in the chapters dealing with whether voluntary organizations are meeting needs and with the subject of institutional renewal, we have tried to be clear about exactly what kinds of groups we are discussing.

Elsewhere we have defined *voluntarism* as those activities and agencies arising out of a spontaneous, private (as contrasted with governmental) effort to promote or advance some aspect of the common good, as this good is perceived by the persons participating in it. These people are *volunteers*—persons who, motivated by varying degrees of altruism and self-interest, choose to give their time and talents freely.[7]

Having worked our way through the definitional thicket we come now to another area of uncertainty—the number of voluntary organizations, the extent of which no one really knows. Using his own definition of a voluntary association as any formal voluntary group and extrapolating from various national and local surveys about numbers of members in voluntary organizations and numbers of such organizations, Smith estimates that there are about 6 million voluntary organizations in the United States.[8] Dixon uses a figure of 7 million voluntary groups in the country, including issue-oriented units, professional societies and so forth.[9] If one turns to those organizations which have been granted tax-exempt status by the Internal Revenue Service, not surprisingly a much smaller group is included. Working from the *Cumulative List of Tax-Exempt Organizations*, The American Association of Fund-Raising Counsel reported to the Coalition for the Public Good in November 1972, the following: 420,000 churches, 2,500 private colleges and universities, 1,000 private secondary schools, 3,386 private nonprofit hospitals, 50,000 health agencies, 30,000 welfare agencies, 5,000 civic and cultural organizations, and 30,000 foundations or family funds.[10] These figures would not include those many groups which, for one reason or another, have never sought or obtained tax-exempt status.

Equally puzzling is the determination of just how many volunteers as well as members of voluntary organizations there are in the United States. Various researchers in the last several years have estimated as high a total as 70 million,[11] and various national organizations have utilized similar numbers. The American Association of Fund-Raising Counsel in the study reported that nearly 70 million Americans give volunteer time to help the programs of the more than 500,000 groups it had included.[12] The National Center for Voluntary Action estimates that 50 to 60 million people belong to volunteer groups of some sort.[13] These estimates did not, however allow for the multiple memberships that many Americans hold and a more definitive and reliable determination of the number of Americans volunteering is to be found in the study, *Americans Volunteer,* completed by the Bureau of the Census for Action, the U.S. government agency which coordinates domestic and international volunteer programs sponsored by the federal government.[14]

Utilizing the results of a survey conducted during April 1974, the Bureau found that one out of every four Americans over the age of thirteen does some form of volunteer work—or approximately 37 million people. What was also extremely interesting was the proportion of persons involved in different types of volunteer activity, again a figure hitherto unknown. Fifty percent of these persons volunteered their services through religious organizations; health and education had equal proportions, each 15 percent; civic and community, 14 percent; citizenship activities, 12 percent; recreational, 11 percent; social welfare, 7 percent; political, 3 percent; and justice (court volunteers, etc.) 1 percent. (These percentages add up to more than 100 percent because the methodology permitted the volunteer to show more than one type of activity.)

What about voluntary giving? Because voluntarism has evolved from its earlier pattern of neighbor directly helping neighbor to more institutionalized forms, voluntary giving is a sensitive barometer of the condition of voluntarism. Fortunately, these data have been systematically reported by the American Association of Fund-Raising Counsel for many years, and are the source of the following details.[15]

Contributions to philanthropy totalled $25.15 billion in 1974, an increase of 106 percent in the decade from 1965, and an increase of 1,912 percent over contributions of $1.25 billion in 1940, the earliest year for which reliable data are available. In constant dollars, of course, the increase is much less: for example, the increase from 1965 to 1974 was 31.8 percent, compared to 106 percent. Nevertheless, the increase in giving, and the gross amount itself, constitute an impressive figure.

As a percentage of gross national product, which increased slightly more than 100 percent in the decade from 1965 to 1974, giving to philanthropy has remained fairly constant. In 1965 the percentage of gross national product was 1.79; this rose to a high of 2.01 in 1971 and declined to 1.80 in 1974.

Where did this money come from? By far the largest amount, $19.8 billion, or 78.7 percent, came from individuals in 1974, an increase of 7.8 percent over the preceding year, and an increase of 13 percent since 1965. It is interesting to note, however, that individual giving, as it relates to personal income and disposable personal income, has remained constant over the past decade. As a proportion of personal income, individual giving was

1.72 percent in 1965, increased to 1.83 percent in 1968 and reverted to the same 1.72 percent in 1974. As a percent of disposable personal income, individual giving began the decade at 1.96 percent, went to 2.14 percent in 1969, and dropped to 2.02 percent in 1974. What these figures suggest is that people's giving habits are remarkably stable and closely linked to income. It also suggests that, in the aggregate, such giving falls far below a sacrificial level, especially since giving for religious purposes is included. For example, as a percent of personal consumption expenditures, giving for religion and welfare in 1972 was reported to be 1.4 percent; expenditures for tobacco for the same year were reported to be 1.7 percent.[16]

The second largest source of income for philanthropy in 1974 was in bequests, which totalled $2.07 billion, up 3.5 percent from the previous year, and up 103 percent by comparison with 1965. This substantial increase is generally attributed to a more systematic and aggressive encouragement of bequests by many philanthropic organizations.

The third largest source of revenue for voluntary philanthropy in 1974 was foundations, which contributed a total of $2.111 billion, or 8.4 percent of all philanthropic giving. This represented a 5 percent increase over the previous year, but was an increase of 87 percent over the decade from 1965 to 1974.

The final source of philanthropic revenue was corporate giving which in 1974 accounted for $1.17 billion, up 10.4 percent over 1973 and representing 4.7 percent of all giving. Under an amendment to the Internal Revenue Code passed in 1935 corporations may contribute to philanthropy up to 5 percent of their profits before taxes. The impact of this law over the past ten years is of interest. Corporate net profits before taxes increased from 1965 to

1974 by 81.7 percent; contributions increased by an estimated 49 percent; and corporate giving as a percent of profits subject to tax decreased by 22 percent. In other words, corporate profits have outstripped increases in giving. It should be noted, however, that corporations contributed to philanthropy in other ways. It has been estimated that the 1974 value of loaned corporate executive time, if deductible at fair market value, would be approximately $50 million; and that the administration of the corporate contribution function in 1974 would have approached $75 million in cost.[17]

Where did the astonishing contribution total of $25.15 billion go in 1974? The largest amount, $10.85 billion, or 43.1 percent, went to religion, up 7.5 percent over the preceding year. Health care and hospitals received $3.90 billion, or 15.5 percent, up 2.6 percent; next was education which received $3.72 billion, or 14.8 percent, approximately the same amount as in 1973; social welfare received $2.34 billion, or 9.3 percent, a figure which was 11.4 percent greater than the preceding year; arts and the humanities received $1.28 billion, or 5.1 percent of the total; civic and public causes received $710 million, or 2.8 percent; and others (foundation endowments, foreign aid, and international affairs) accounted for $2.35 billion, or 9.4 percent, and were down 21.1 percent from the previous year, as a percent of all giving.

The trends in giving to health care and social welfare are of particular interest. Giving to health and hospitals totalled $2.08 billion in 1965 and rose to $3.90 billion at the end of the following decade, an increase of 88 percent. During this period the health and hospitals share of all philanthropic giving remained fairly constant: 17 percent in 1965 and 15.5 percent in 1974. Contributions and bequests to twenty-one of the largest national voluntary health agencies totalled $458 million in 1974, an increase of about 9 percent over 1973.

Giving to social welfare increased from $860 million in 1965 to $2.34 billion in 1974, an increase of 172 percent. The share of all giving to social welfare was 7 percent in 1965; 9.3 percent in 1974. It is of interest to note that contributions to social welfare purposes were a much higher percentage of all giving in the 1940s and 1950s. For example, in 1940 contributions for social welfare were 16 percent of the total of all contributions; in 1945 the figure was 24.5 percent (doubtless affected by wartime needs); in 1950 the amount was 19.4 percent; and in 1958 the percentage had declined to 18.3.[18]

Voluntarism, the activities of voluntary organizations across the length and breadth of the land, occupying the time, the talents and the dedication of, at the very least, a quarter of our total adult population, and supported by more than 25 billion dollars a year for every type of civic, charitable, educational, and cultural endeavor—this indeed is a significant phenomenon in American life today. Can we afford to simply step aside in the face of forces which would change its character, weaken its impact on our social and cultural institutions, and noticeably impede the forward thrust of this movement which is both part and parcel of our democratic process and a reflection of the finest aspirations of the human spirit? To this question we will next address ourselves.

NOTES

1. HERBERT H. HYMAN and CHARLES R. WRIGHT, "Trends in Voluntary Association Memberships of American Adults: Replication Based on Secondary Analysis of National Sample Surveys," *American Sociological Review,* 36 (April 1971), pp. 191–206. *Contra*, NICHOLAS BABCHUK, and ALAN BOOTH, "Voluntary Association Membership: A Longitudinal Analysis," *American Sociological Review,* 34 (February 1969), pp. 31–45.

2. JAMES CURTIS, "Voluntary Association Joining: A Cross-National Comparative Note," *American Sociological Review,* 36 (October 1971), pp. 872–880. Drawing upon secondary analysis of data from the U.S. and five other democratic societies, Curtis illustrates this rather tellingly.

3. Ibid. and cf. J.A. WILLIAMS, JR., "Voluntary Associations and Minority Status: A Comparative Analysis of Anglo, Black, and Mexican Americans," *American Sociological Review,* 38 (October 1973), pp. 637–646; D.J. VORWALLER, "Social Mobility and Membership in Voluntary Associations," *American Journal of Sociology,* 75 (January 1970), pp. 481–495.

4. DAVID HORTON SMITH, "A Survey of the Voluntary Sector in a Single Community" (report for the National Center for Voluntary Action transmitted to the Commission on Private Philanthropy and Public Needs, January 13, 1975).

5. ALAN PIFER, "The Jeopardy of Private Institutions," *Annual Report for 1970* (New York: Carnegie Corporation, 1970), p. 3.

6. W.K. WARNER and S.M. MILLER, "Organizational Problems in Two Types of Voluntary Associations", *American Journal of Sociology,* 69 (May, 1964), pp. 654–657.

7. The problems created in such a definition by the payment

of volunteers through the various Action programs will be dealt with in the next chapter.

8. DAVID HORTON SMITH, ed., "Voluntary Associations and Volunteering in the United States," *Voluntary Action Research 1974: Voluntary Action Around the World* (Boston: Lexington Books, 1974), p. 282.

9. "50,000,000 Helping Hands," *U.S. News and World Report* (September 2, 1970).

10. American Association of Fund-Raising Counsel, Inc., John J. Schwartz, President, *Report to the Coalition for the Public Good* (New York: American Association of Fund-Raising Counsel, Inc., 1972).

11. DAVID HORTON SMITH, ed., op. cit., p. 219.

12. American Association of Fund-Raising Counsel, Inc., op. cit.

13. "50,000,000 Helping Hands," op. cit.

14. The Agency for Volunteer Service, *Americans Volunteer 1974,* (Washington, D.C.: Action, 1975).

15. American Association of Fund-Raising Counsel, Inc., *1975 Annual Report,* (New York: American Association of Fund-Raising Counsel, Inc., 1975).

16. LAURENCE URDANG, ed., *The Official Associated Press Almanac 1975,* (Maplewood, N.J.: Hammond Almanac, Inc., 1975).

17. WILLIAM TURNER, Executive Director, National Conference on Philanthropy (oral statement at the 501 (C) (3) Group meeting, January 9, 1975).

18. *Voluntary Health and Welfare Agencies in the United States* (New York: Schoolmasters' Press, 1961).

3 THE VOLUNTEER
AND THE PROFESSIONAL

NO DISCUSSION OF voluntarism can proceed far without some examination of the two essential human components of every type of voluntary organization—the volunteer and the professional. Is every member of a voluntary organization a "volunteer"? Does every type of voluntary group develop a professional corps?

To answer the first question we turn once again to Smith who has endowed the field of voluntarism with a most helpful typology of volunteers, which aided these authors in leaping over an otherwise insurmountable conceptual hurdle. In *Volunteer Administration,*[1] Smith, focusing on broad types of goals, both individual and social, and various kinds of psychic benefits and rewards, defined five main categories of volunteers:

1. *Service volunteers,* the traditional "people helping people" group who attempt to help others directly and who in terms of the organizational context in which they work may be sub-defined into a) those in institutional programs (e.g., churches, prisons, schools), b) those in autonomous service groups (e.g., Red Cross), c) those in self-help groups (e.g., drug programs, welfare rights programs).

2. *Public issue/advocacy volunteers,* those persons whose concern is with the social, economic and political roots of problems for large groups of people, and who, depending on their

primary interest, may be either a) public information volunteers, b) political campaign
workers, c) public issue volunteers or d) rights
advocacy volunteers.

3. *Consummatory/self-expressive volunteers,* who
generally appeal not to altruistic motivation
but to some self interest usually emphasizing
fellowship, fun, enjoyment, and which may be
sub-divided into a) cultural/esthetics volunteers, b) social club members, c) recreational
club members and d) hobby and games club
members.

4. *Occupational/economic self-interest volunteers,*
again like the third category self-oriented but
which seek to protect and enhance their occu-
pational and/or economic interests, the while
they may at the same time engage in programs
beneficial to the community as a whole;
among these are a) professional association
members, b) businessmen's and civic association members and c) labor union members.

5. *Fund-raising volunteers* who are primarily involved in the process of raising funds and who
may be either a) general fund-raising volunteers (e.g., a United Fund worker) or b) specific fund-raising volunteers.

For anyone attempting to view voluntarism in its broadest
perspective we consider the foregoing classification to be
a signal contribution and agree with Smith's conclusion:

When a broad view of voluntarism is taken, the
major kinds of volunteers that can be identified
are much more varied than usually considered

under the heading of "volunteer" . . . a full and complete picture of volunteers and voluntarism cannot ignore all of the facets discussed briefly above.

When people speak of "voluntarism," they often have in mind only one subtype of the typology presented here. They say "voluntarism" but *really* mean only "service oriented voluntarism," or they really mean only "issue/advocacy voluntarism." Although these latter two types of voluntarism are probably the most *crucial* types of voluntarism in terms of unique functions for society, they are not *all* that is worth considering in the realm of voluntarism.[2]

While much of what follows hereafter will indeed focus on service-oriented and issue-advocacy volunteers and voluntarism, we consider that no discussion of voluntarism would be adequate without recognition that the exciting panoply which it encompasses in our nation arises from the diverse needs, interests, desires, and goals which have led to the creation of every type of group imaginable, and enriched the lives of all of us. (We are not oblivious, however, to those groups and organizations without which the nation would surely have been better off!)

That professionals are equally indispensable to voluntarism today cannot be gainsaid. Some of the earliest professions grew from the first impulses to help others—medicine, law, religion, education. Others, like social work and nursing, were of later origin. Today there is no field of voluntary endeavor which does not possess a skilled cadre of paid workers—the caseworker, the community organizer, the hospital administrator, the college president, the fund raiser, the union organizer. The increasingly complex nature of many volunteer groups and voluntary organizations coupled with the vast explosion of scientific, technical and humane knowledge, has necessitated the development of "operators" of the culture systems, trained, competent and committed individuals who give their paid services as specialists to the groups and organizations for which they work.

Specialization has augmented the demand for training both of professionals and volunteers. Every major profession has a vast array of subspecialties, the preparation for which may take months or even years. Concomitantly, many of the voluntary groups, but especially those which are service- or public issue-oriented may demand of their volunteers intensive training and high degrees of skill. This is but a logical step in the institutionalization of volunteering which has, like professionalization, moved at an ever-accelerating pace in the past century. Citizen leaders of the early Charity Organization Societies recognized the impossibility of all of their investigatory work being done by volunteers and used paid agents. They found that

> To find out the real needs of the poor, and to form and carry out a plan which . . . should lead to their restoration . . . required not only patience and intelligence and a genuine interest, but *practical training, constructive ability and a willingness to subordinate the immediate good to a future better.* [emphasis added][3]

In 1898 the New York Charity Organization Society began its first training course for prospective agency workers, a summer program which led in a few years to its expansion into a one-year program given by the New York School of Philanthropy, the forerunner of the New York School of Social Work. This same period saw the inauguration of educational programs for "social workers" in a number of cities around the country.[4] A new profession was born.

But even earlier, it was the birth of the National Council of Jewish Women which brought the first organized approach to the recruitment and training of volunteers, offering programs to train young women for philanthropic work and pioneering new services for other public and voluntary agencies.[5] Other organizations of the early twentieth century followed suit and some among them, notably the Association of Junior Leagues, the League of Women Voters and the American Red Cross, have been outstanding for the breadth and scope of their training programs down to the present. Today, there is no major voluntary organization making extensive use of volunteers which does not have a comprehensive training program for them.

Yet it is the use of the service-oriented and the public issue- (change-) oriented volunteer which in recent years has been a persistent cause of tension within many voluntary organizations, especially those "established" organizations with a predominance of paid staff. Normally, in such organizations the volunteers are the members of the boards of directors with greater or lesser degrees of control over the management of the agencies. Whether there is also a function for them in the actual operation of the program has been dependent on a number of variables: (1) the attitude of the executive and staff toward their use, (2) the type of activity in which the organization is engaged, and (3) the need for their service.

This was not always so. In, for example, the social

welfare organizations of the turn of the century, the social work profession was in its infancy and the earlier work of the Charity Organization Societies had led to joint efforts between the lay and the paid workers, both in treatment of individual cases of poverty, neglect, and family breakdown, and in efforts at social and legislative reform. Their joint success in improvement of housing conditions, prevention of tuberculosis, establishment of juvenile courts, child labor laws, workers' compensation laws, and many others produced what has been called the "Golden Era of Social Legislation."[6]

The decade of the 1920s saw the social work profession become introspective as it strove to incorporate new psychological insights into developing professional practices. This preoccupation provided limited scope for the activities of volunteers, other than as board members, and diminished concern for social reform. Indeed, voices were raised questioning the need for boards and the significance of volunteer contributions, other than monetary, to social welfare. The massive efforts required to bring relief to millions during the Depression, however, once again signalled the importance of volunteers' work, and the mobilization of the American public during the Second World War brought an estimated eleven million volunteers into every type of volunteer service, including those more recently reserved for the professional. In the aftermath of the war there was a renewed emphasis on professionalism and once more a retrenchment in the functions assigned to volunteers. In many agencies, only the most menial tasks of typing, answering the phone, carrying trays, and similar work was given to the volunteer, regardless of his or her background, education, or experience.[7] We are reminded of a friend, an ex-executive of a large city social agency, who after retirement, went on the board of another agency and who commented that she was appalled at the attitude now expressed toward any of her ideas because she was a "volunteer."

The last fifteen years have seen a variety of new patterns emerge for voluntarism, each with implications for the service-oriented and public issue- (change-) oriented volunteer and voluntary organization. We will deal again in later chapters with several of these patterns but they must be mentioned at this point. The first is the difficult situation in which so many organizations and agencies, both local and national find themselves as sources of funds fail to keep pace with the demands for service. Is it then appropriate to add volunteers to paid professional staff or replace those who are lost through attrition with volunteers? What is the resultant effect on staff morale? But alternatively, if the service is valuable to the community, should it not be performed even at the sacrifice of a certain professionalism? This last is a most difficult question to phrase, much less to answer. And if a service is valuable to the community why can it not be paid for?—a question we shall look at later in this chapter.

The second pattern, so important as to justify its separate treatment in another chapter, is the revived emphasis on social reform, social action, and advocacy for the improvement of the economic and social conditions which contribute to family breakdown, delinquency, unemployment, discrimination, poor housing, and alienation. Here, renewed scope for the activity of the volunteer is found in the extension of education, health, social welfare, and cultural goals into the community through a variety of outlets including legislation, public relations, the pressures of power groups and of informal power situations (the "reserve of influence" discussed later). Charles Schottland, writing in 1961, prophesied the necessity for such a volunteer commitment:

> For the past twenty years or more we have
> focussed much attention on the respective roles of
> the volunteer and the professional. But this atten-
> tion has been related primarily to analyzing what
> are professional and what are volunteer tasks
> . . . If voluntary agencies will emphasize their
> contribution to public social policy, they can vi-
> talize many of our volunteer activities and give to
> volunteers a sense of real participation in broad
> community problems.[8]

More than this, as Levin pointed out in 1969, the citizens
who sit as board members of an agency comprise a powerful area of authority for social change.[9] Though he was
referring specifically to social agencies, we see this as true
of all major voluntary organizations that are in any way
other-serving groups, and we would extend the concept to
embrace members as well as program volunteers in any of
these groups.

Still another and probably the most critical issue
which has emerged in relation to volunteering is the
changing role of the woman volunteer. With many more
options open to her—school, employment, opportunities
for career advancement—will she continue the traditional
role she has played since the Civil War of service- and
fund-raising volunteer? Though the study by Action,
which in part compares figures from a 1965 study of
volunteering with those of 1974, shows during this period
a slightly higher proportionate increase in numbers of men
volunteering (from 15 to 20 percent of the population, a
gain of 33⅓ percent, while that of women increased from
21 to 26 percent, a gain of only 23.8 percent), the fact
remains that at the present the most typical American
volunteer is still a married, white woman between ages 25
and 44 who holds a college degree and is in the upper-

income bracket.[10] Whether this will remain the pattern of succeeding decades is highly debatable. Moreover, a fundamental question has been raised by the National Organization of Women (NOW) which, if not answered in the negative, may have a chilling effect on the numbers of female volunteers in the service area.

NOW, in a 1974 conference resolution, said women should be only change-oriented volunteers, and disapproved of the service volunteer on the ground that such service was nothing more than an exploitation of women designed to keep them in a subordinate position. It advanced the argument that these services performed by women are needed by society and should therefore be paid for by society. If women refused to do them, society would have to pay and thus the status of women would be enhanced. A chorus of voices in opposition to this position, including those of the president of the Association of Junior Leagues, Mary Poole, the president of the National Council of Negro Women, Dorothy Height, and the chairperson of Call for Action, Ellen Sulzberger Strauss, all outstanding volunteers themselves, defended the position of the woman service volunteer and her freedom of choice, a choice which they suggested NOW was attempting to eliminate. Height says that one has to work in both directions, social service and change:

> While you work to open the doors, you have to salvage the talents, interests and spirits of people so that they will be ready to walk through these doors.[11]

Strauss pointed to the many tasks that would simply go undone were they not performed by volunteers. And Poole makes the telling comment that

> I don't think you find NOW saying that a man
> shouldn't serve as a Big Brother to a ghetto boy
> who wouldn't otherwise know any men. I doubt
> you'd find NOW saying that a man shouldn't
> coach his son's Young America Football team.
> It's not service volunteering that degrades
> women; on the contrary, it's the prevailing atti-
> tude toward women that is degrading service
> volunteering . . .

She concludes that

> It is my hunch that once the objectives of the
> women's movement are achieved, NOW will not
> object to women being service volunteers (or any-
> thing else they want to be) and this reinforces my
> belief that it's not really volunteering that is the
> culprit.[12]

At this writing it is much too soon to assess the potential
effects of the philosophical position taken by NOW. What
we do see, as born out by the Action survey, are increasing
numbers of volunteers of every age, income bracket, and
education level, nonwhite and white, men, women, students, retired persons—an enormous fund of time and
talent—who appear to look beyond economic concerns to
other values and goals to which they are committing
themselves.[13] In great part this has been due to the various
so-called liberation movements of the sixties, many of
them springing from groupings of voluntary associations,
united around critical issues, which have effectively
brought new insights, values, and modes of operation to
bear on those issues. The two decades of the sixties and the
seventies will certainly be known as the era of citizen
participation. We shall return to this theme later.

We could not conclude this chapter without mentioning two other developing patterns whose importance cannot yet be evaluated. The first of these has been the creation of Action, a federal agency which coordinates all government-related volunteer programs and has brought together a number of widely scattered agencies, including the Peace Corps, VISTA, the Retired Senior Volunteer Program (RSVP), the Service Corps of Retired Executives (SCORE) and the National Student Volunteer Program.[14] The significance of Action has been in its support of volunteers with training, transportation, out-of-pocket expense money, and in some cases (the full-time Peace Corps and VISTA workers) a subsistence allowance leading to their designation as quasi-volunteers. Particularly for students, older persons, and persons of low-income levels this support has made possible their participation as volunteers in growing numbers, and has raised the practical question for voluntary organizations of whether and to what extent volunteers should be reimbursed for expenses connected with volunteering, especially if, as we believe desirable, access to volunteering is to be open to all socioeconomic groups.

In view of the straitened circumstances of so many voluntary organizations at this juncture in history the question may be purely academic. Local service agencies already forced by inflation to cut back program and services can hardly afford postage, telephone, or lunch money for volunteers. Major national organizations which must pare staff and projects cannot reimburse board members for travel expenses, thus reducing the effectiveness of those board members who cannot otherwise afford to attend meetings at great distances from their homes. We would propose that, ideally, all volunteers be reimbursed for their out-of-pocket expenses when engaged in activities for tax-exempt organizations.

This raises the allied question of the tax deductibility of unreimbursed expenses, some of which are permissible under present Internal Revenue Code Regulations (such as telephone, travel, meals when away overnight, uniforms when required), and others of which are not deductible (such as child care expenses and meals if one is not away overnight).[15] Future policy decisions in this area will presumably have a bearing on entrance into volunteer positions for many.

Another matter which is the subject of increasing discussion and of legislative proposals is that of tax benefits for volunteer time. With some variations, proposals would permit the volunteer to take a certain amount of volunteer time, multiply it by the minimum wage, and claim the resulting amount (or a part of it) as a deduction or a tax credit. The issues raised are complex. One argument by proponents is that of equity: the well-to-do can now make a dollar contribution, which gives rise to a tax deduction; the less well-to-do can give time, but receive no monetary advantage. The proposal would permit low-income persons to give time, and receive some benefit on their tax returns. A second argument is that such an action would afford well-deserved recognition, by the government and the people, of the important services which volunteers provide. A question may be raised, however, as to whether the plan would really provide an incentive for persons from all socioeconomic groups to volunteer. An even more difficult question is to judge the long-range effect of linking volunteer service to a tax benefit. Does anything happen to commitment if the volunteer becomes money oriented?

Proponents of the proposals argue that a tax benefit for volunteer time would have an affirmative impact upon recruitment and retention of volunteers. However, administering such a program would create serious problems of paperwork for organizations, especially when it is considered that many volunteers serve more than one organization. There is also an inherent difficulty in equitably valuing a volunteer's time. Either everyone's time is valued the same (which may be unrealistic) or time is valued at market value, which is virtually impossible. One final question which requires careful study is the revenue impact of the proposal. Depending upon the tax credit formula used, the revenue consequences of tax credit proposals could be substantial, and it is important that these be understood.

This book is about the crossroads at which voluntarism finds itself. Like voluntarism generally, the role, status, supply, and perhaps the sense of commitment of volunteers seem to be in process of change. The changing composition of volunteers found in the Action survey noted above is confirmed by a recent survey of volunteers in Canada.[16] A 1975 study by the Canadian Council on Social Development, *Volunteers: The Untapped Potential,* shows that in Canada some 44.5 percent of volunteers are men; people of all ages are involved, with substantial representation of people under 25 and over 60; and with some 48 percent reporting family incomes of less than $12,000 per year. Reuben Baetz, executive director of the Council, says: "The study shatters the stereotyped image about volunteers and voluntarism and casts a surprising ray of hope on what is frequently regarded as our increasingly alienated and impersonal society. . . . The traditional image of the volunteer, as a bored, middle-aged housewife with time on her hands, lots of money and zealous desire to do good, is outdated . . ."[16] These trends augur well for the future of volunteers in both Canada and the United States.

But it is incumbent upon us to understand and influence some of the forces that will accelerate or retard these important developments: the impact of inflation, which makes it impossible for some to volunteer without reimbursement of out-of-pocket expenses; the unpredictable influence of the women's movement, which is making it possible for many educated women to go to work in preference to doing volunteer activity; and, finally, the intangible but crucial relationship of the volunteer to the professional. When volunteers have other options for constructive activity it is not likely that they will welcome being "put down" by thoughtless professionals, as is sometimes the case.

We believe that everyone understands that voluntarism, as we know it, would collapse overnight if all volunteers were to withdraw from their myriad activities. What may not be so widely understood is the incalculable damage that would follow a declining trend in the numbers of volunteers. Hence arises the importance of wide discussion and dialogue on such public policy issues as payment of out-of-pocket expenses, the allowance of tax deductions for such expenses, and the more controversial issue of the deduction of volunteer time. What would be the impact of each of these proposed measures upon the recruitment and retention of volunteers? Perhaps of even greater importance over time will be the attitude of the professional. Will he or she recognize the importance of the role of the volunteer, and accord it the status which it deserves, within a collegial relationship which provides assurance to the volunteer of his or her worth?

NOTES

1. DAVID HORTON SMITH, "Types of Volunteers and Voluntary Action," *Volunteer Administration,* July 1972, pp. 3–10.
2. Ibid., pp. 9–10.
3. MARY CONYNGTON, *How to Help: A Manual of Practical Charity,* p. 11. As cited by Herman Levin, "Volunteers in Social Welfare: The Challenge of their Future," *Social Work,* January 1969, p. 86.
4. RACHEL B. MARKS, "Education for Social Work," *Encyclopedia of Social Work,* 15th ed., p. 277.
5. VIOLET M. SIEDER, "Volunteers," *Encyclopedia of Social Work,* 15th ed., p. 831.
6. HERMAN LEVIN, "Volunteers in Social Welfare: The Challenge of Their Future," *Social Work,* January 1969, p. 87.
7. SIEDER, op. cit., p. 831. Cf. D.G. BECKER, "Exit Lady Bountiful: The Volunteer and the Professional Social Worker," *Social Service Review,* 38 (March 1964), pp. 57–72.
8. CHARLES I. SCHOTTLAND, "The Exercise of Communal Leadership—Relationship and Roles of the Professional and Volunteer," *Journal of Jewish Communal Service,* 38 (Fall 1961), p. 107. As cited by Herman Levin, op. cit., p. 93.
9. LEVIN, op. cit., p. 93.
10. The Agency for Volunteer Service, *Americans Volunteer 1974,* (Washington, D.C.: Action, 1975), p. 3.
11. ENID NEMY, "NOW Attacks Volunteerism—But Others Rally To Its Defense," *New York Times,* 7 June 1974, p. 41.
12. "The Association of Junior Leagues' Position on Voluntarism" (statement by MARY POOLE, President of the Association of Junior Leagues, New York).
13. The Agency for Volunteer Service, op. cit., pp. 12–13.

14. For an excellent synopsis of the Action program, cf. DAVID HORTON SMITH, ed., "Voluntary Associations and Volunteering in the United States," *Voluntary Action Research 1974: Voluntary Action Around the World* (Boston: Lexington Books, 1974), pp. 296–297.

15. Cf. Internal Revenue Service, Rev. Rul. 73–597, 1973 *Cum. Bul.* (December 31, 1973).

16. NOVIA CARTER, *Volunteers: The Untapped Potential* (Ottawa: Canadian Council on Social Development, 1975).

PART II

EXTERNAL FORCES
AND THEIR IMPACT
ON VOLUNTARISM

The viability of voluntary organizations in the next quarter century will depend upon the impact—for good or for ill—of such wholly external phenomena as governmental regulation, the movement toward tax reform, the extent of permissible legislative activity, and the potential for adequate funding. Public policy and support in these areas will require a broad base of citizen understanding, confidence, and support.

4 THE HEAVY HAND
OF REGULATION

BEYOND ANY DOUBT one of the most complex questions affecting the voluntary sector is the extent of necessary regulation. The following excerpt from a memorandum from Charles Sampson, Chairman, to members of the 501 (c) (3) Group, an informal assemblage of executives and fund raisers of major national philanthropic organizations, notes this problem:

> Setting standards for and informing the contributing public about organizational adherence to them is a very complex matter. Even if every organization were in total compliance, the contributing public would not automatically be assured that this was a fact. Nor can standards be effectively applied by the average citizen on a do-it-yourself basis. They are certainly not self-policing.
>
> Standards which focus exclusively on fiscal honesty and truth in advertising cannot do the complete job. An organization may be totally inept in its chosen field and yet if it is fiscally honest and truthful, it might well pass muster. This, however, does not mean it ought to be supported.[1]

What is the function of regulation? The answer is perhaps best stated by the following excerpt from a paper by Norris E. Class, *The Regulatory Challenge to Social Work:*

> In the final analysis, the basic function . . . of regulation is the mediating of two conflicting sets of rights. One set is the right of persons—all persons—to certain fundamental safeguards as consumers or users of those products or services which result from private action or enterprise and which are deemed to have a public interest. The other set relates to the rights of persons to engage in private enterprise: to do their own thing whether that thing is running a factory, business, bank, a commercial day care center, or a privately sponsored philanthropic facility for the elderly. In short, a regulatory activity always endeavors to mediate the two sets of rights—those of the producer of a service or product and those of a consumer of the service or product.[2]

Historically, the function of regulation is derived from the common law doctrine of *parens patriae,* which had its origin in England and which is defined as the power of the sovereign as parent of the country to protect the interests of those citizens who are incapable of protecting themselves (children, lunatics, dependents, and charitable beneficiaries). In England this doctrine became what could more accurately be described as the inherent jurisdiction of Courts of Chancery over all charities. Thus, the English system of common law regulation and enforcement of charitable dispositions by the Attorney-General on behalf of beneficiaries (i.e., the public) was transferred to America.

It was not, however, until the decades of the 1940s and 1950s that any impetus was given to the development of statutory law at the state level. One contributing development occurred when the National Conference of Com-

missioners on Uniform State Laws proposed in 1954 a
model registration and reporting act entitled "The Uniform Supervision of Trustees for Charitable Purposes
Act." Even so, there are now only thirteen states which
require registration and only fifteen which require annual
reporting to the Attorney General.[3]

The above cited article has this to say about the
status of regulation at the local level:

> The regulation of charitable trusts and founda-
> tions is even less organized on the local level than
> on the state level. Due to the fact that very few
> records are kept and there is very little coordina-
> tion of effort, it is practically impossible to deter-
> mine what role local municipalities play in the
> overall regulation of charitable trusts and founda-
> tions. At best, the regulatory role of municipali-
> ties can be characterized as sporadic.[4]

Meanwhile, various processes of self-regulation
have been taking place within the voluntary sector, many
antedating the statutory regulation by public authorities.
Accreditation mechanisms within the fields of health, education, and welfare, and review processes, such as those of
the National Information Bureau and the Council of Better Business Bureaus, have done a great deal to establish
and advance standards.

Today, the proposal that there be some new form
of federal regulation makes it necessary for all these developments to be placed in a perspective of what form regulation of voluntarism shall take and under whose auspices
it shall occur. Perhaps another way of stating the same
perspective is to ask, Who will decide on the future role

of philanthropy? Will it be government; givers, including foundations and corporations; consumers, including youth and minority groups; professionals; or public opinion generally? Whichever group it may be, one's whole concept and philosophy of voluntarism will be tested as this debate goes forward in the near future. Issues of accountability, control, standards, fund-raising, performance, consumerism, and freedom are just some of the standards to which one must repair as the dialogue is carried forward.

Governmental regulation is here to stay and will predictably increase in the future. There are far too many forces at play to hold that it will either stop where it is or just "go away." For one thing, there is the size and scope of voluntary effort. With voluntary contributions in excess of 25 billion dollars, with volunteers numbering (about) 40 million persons, and with 226,122 voluntary organizations reported in the 501 (c) (3) category by the Internal Revenue Service, it can readily be seen that the voluntary enterprise is "big business." Its effective and ethical functioning properly becomes a matter of wide concern, whether one be a contributor, a consumer, or a concerned citizen. Moreover, there have been a few spectacular instances of abuse, or alleged abuse, which have received wide press coverage, and which have led some to believe that "where there is smoke there is fire." There is no field of activity which has, or should have, higher standards of fiduciary responsibility than the voluntary sector, and where this has been breached in any degree the movement toward great public control and regulation is irresistible.

An additional factor in the march toward greater public regulation is the concept of "tax expenditure." As we shall see in the next chapter this is the concept that revenue losses to the federal government attributable to the effect of the deduction for charitable contributions are deemed to be tax expenditures. It is but a short step to the conclusion that the federal government thus has some responsibility for concern and control over how that money shall be spent. In our view there are better rationales for government regulation than the application of the tax expenditure concept but, nevertheless, it is a theory which appears to be gaining ground, and one which may well influence public policy in the future. Finally, concern for the voluntary sector seems, to some extent, to be cyclical. The Gunn-Platt Survey of 1945; the report, *Voluntary Health and Welfare Agencies in the United States,* issued in 1961; the report, *Foundations, Private Giving and Public Policy,* issued in 1969; and now the report of the Commission on Private Philanthropy and Public Needs are all responsive to periodic upsurges of public concern of one kind or another. The Tax Reform Act of 1969 represented, in our view, an overreaction to these periodic concerns, but the few abuses which it was intended to correct tended to contaminate, in people's minds, all of voluntarism. And voluntary organizations are not immune from the widespread lack of confidence which presently afflicts almost all of our institutions, whether public or private.

Hence our concern that the leadership within the voluntary sector not spend time bewailing the fact of governmental control, but address itself to how a system of regulation can be devised which will further the goals and objectives of both the public and the voluntary sectors. And in order to take that constructive step there must be full, open, and candid discussion of the issues which are intrinsically involved.

One of the first, and most troublesome issues, is how to achieve a balance between reasonable regulatory requirements and overkill. The problem is intrinsic because provisions of the law are aimed at the very small percentage of organizations whose behavior falls outside legal or ethical standards. For the vast majority of organizations compliance is burdensome and costly.

The Tax Reform Act of 1969, in its impact on foundations, is a good example of overkill in at least two of its provisions. One example has to do with the 4 percent tax on net investment income, intended to defray the costs to the Internal Revenue Service of audits of foundations required by the Act. From January 1, 1970 to June 30, 1973 a total of $175 million was collected, while a total of only $53 million was spent on foundation audits. In fact the cost to the IRS of auditing all exempt organizations during this period of time came to only $100 million. The unexpended balance of the money collected went into general revenues of the government. In our view this provision is punitive, confiscatory, and objectionable in principle, but efforts to bring the 4 percent tax provisions of the law into conformity with actual costs of audit (in respect to which there is no objection) have proven unsuccessful.

The payout requirements of TRA 69 also seem to us to represent overkill. The Act provided that foundations pay out annually the greater of 1) their current net income, or 2) a fixed "minimum investment return," the latter being set at 6 percent of asset value. One of the reasons for this particular provision was the contention that, relative to their total assets, foundations generally ". . . are not providing an adequate payout to society in return for the immediate tax deductions society has given their donors."[5] It was thought that by imposing some relatively high minimum distribution requirements on foundations they would be impelled to improve investment performance by diversifying their portfolios and increasing their yields, which by the same token would require them to relinquish concentrations of asset holdings in a single class of stock in a single company, and which would result in their increasing their distributions to charitable institutions.

The fallacy of this line of reasoning has been clearly brought out in an article, "The Impact of the Minimum Distribution Rule on Foundations," by Norman D. Ture, who concludes:

> To the extent that public policy calls for a continuing and growing distribution capacity by foundations over the long term, a minimum distribution rule is counterproductive, irrespective of the total rate of return on foundation assets. The higher the required minimum distribution rate, the greater the likelihood of required reduction in foundation corpus, the effect of which on long-term distribution capacity is likely to outweigh by far any increase in rate of return which may be realized by changing the composition of the remaining corpus . . .
>
> The present six percent minimum distribution rule obviously does not take these considerations into account. For a great many foundations, it will require a sharp deceleration in the growth of their distributions. And for any foundation with a rate of return of less than 6.5 percent, it will result in reduction and eventual exhaustion of assets and an absolute decline in the amount of distributions.[6]

Henry Suhrke, in the November 1974 issue of *The Philanthropy Monthly,* notes:

> With the invasions of capital already taking place, it is easy to see the disastrous consequences

that could occur in the next twelve months (if the payout level were to be increased to 7 percent) . . .

We learn the basic folk wisdom of the human race through fairy tales. The moral of the payout controversy is to be found in a fairy tale which legislators ought to re-read. It is the story of killing the goose that laid the golden egg.[7]

Another case of the overkill dilemma is seen in Senator Walter F. Mondale's proposed Truth in Contributions Act introduced in 1975 (an identical bill was introduced in the House by Congressman Joseph E. Karth). The Mondale bill contains two major thrusts in the direction of accountability:

1. A charitable spending control provision which would require certain public charities to use at least 50 percent of their gross revenue for charitable purposes each year.
2. A charitable solicitation reporting control provision which would require charities to file certain reports with IRS and with certain state agencies in addition to those now required and to publish notices of the availability of such reports for inspection by anyone.[8]

The spending control provision simply provides that if an organization's expenses are broken down into management, fund raising, and service, expenditures for service must equal 50 percent of the total. The 50 percent provision is applied to gross revenue, thereby raising some interesting questions. What about donor restricted revenue, the proceeds of which may deliberately be deferred; what about revenue which is, by board action, diverted to purposes such as research projects which may have a life of two or three years; and what about the proceeds from a capital campaign, which would be expended over a longer period of time? But putting aside for a moment the matter of deferred expenditures, and assuming, as is the case in the vast majority of reputable charities, that gross revenue and expenditures are in reasonable balance, it would require a most unusual combination of circumstances for an organization's expenditures for management and general purposes and for fund raising to exceed 50 percent of the budget (thus sending services below 50 percent). And yet it is a fact, and the evidence is to be found in the report of the Hearings before the Subcommittee on Children and Youth, of the Committee on Labor and Public Welfare, U.S. Senate (Senator Mondale, chairman), of instances of excessive fund-raising costs and other expenditures constituting deliberate fraud or misrepresentation in which the donor and the intended beneficiary are both victimized. An instance can be cited in which only six percent of the funds raised by one organization were spent on services; in another the figure for services was seven percent of funds raised; and in one instance fund-raising costs totalled 46.5 percent of funds raised.

The reporting requirements under the solicitation control section of the bill are worthy of note, especially for organizations that feel they already spend too much time filling in forms and reports. The bill requires organizations to submit to the IRS two additional copies of their financial reports, and to file an annual report with each state Attorney General. In addition, organizations must advertise that their annual report is available for inspection and distribution at their offices; and they must offer full financial disclosure to the public at the time of solicitation, regardless of when or how the solicitation is made. Organizations must also make available within fifteen days their disclosure statements to anyone requesting them. These requirements are similar to the new federal Real Estate Settlement Procedures Act of 1975 (RESPA), making mandatory the advance disclosure of all costs in residential transactions, with a view to protecting the consumer. (The majority of the provisions of RESPA have since been rescinded, due to the enormity of the additional burden it put on borrowers, lenders, attorneys, and real estate agents. Instead of protecting the consumer the result was only increased cost and aggravation. The analogy here is self-evident.) That the Treasury would encourage state Attorneys General to accept copies of forms submitted to the IRS rather than require separate filings in each state only emphasizes the importance of some system of uniformity and reciprocity in reporting among the states, and between them and the federal government.

In addition to the Mondale bill, Congressman Lionel Van Deerlin introduced in 1975 the Truth in Giving Bill. The objective of this proposal is to make it easier for donors to identify charity charlatans before contributing to the "causes" for which they solicit. The measure would require any organization which uses any instrumentality of interstate commerce (mail, telephone, telegraph, radio, television) to solicit contributions, to respond to requests for information from anyone seeking it.

Compliance with both the Mondale and Van Deerlin bills would be burdensome and expensive. The former would exempt churches, private schools and colleges, hospitals, service clubs, civic groups, and veterans organizations. The Van Deerlin bill would exempt only churches, private schools and colleges. So the issue of the desirable balance in public policy between necessary regulation and overkill remains. How can we regulate the few without onerous impositions on all organizations, the smaller and poorer of which may be forced out of business? Yet another way to look at the problem is to observe that the cost of invoking the police power to control the few is ultimately to benefit the many and in theory must be borne by the many—in this case those organizations whose reputations are adversely affected by the wrongdoing of the few who would defraud the public.

A second, and even more difficult issue within the whole field of regulation is that of a desirable balance between governmental and voluntary, or self-regulatory efforts. The accomplishments of both the public and private sectors represent a mixed pattern. A recent authoritative survey of self-regulation conducted by Peter Meek for the Commission on Private Philanthropy and Public Needs makes the following general observation:

> During this study several persons expressed the opinion that self-regulation by the private sector, including philanthropy, is a myth in the United States. It is a concept which the private sector believes in, practices, and behind which it rallies when the threat of governmental intervention is perceived. The contrary view of other authorities claims that public regulation, as exemplified by the major Federal regulating bodies in trade, transportation, etc. and by the state licensing bodies, is captured by the vested interests in the private sector very soon after the public regulatory body is created, if, indeed, the enabling legislation has not already built in private control of the public function.
>
> The descriptions of existing self-regulatory

mechanisms in private philanthropy in this report do not necessarily confirm such a cynical viewpoint. The report is a recital of impressive concern and sincere interest in self-regulation by the private sector. At the same time, it is apparent that the effectiveness of any of the efforts described—or the cumulative effectiveness of all—as devices to regulate philanthropy in the sense of assuring appropriate use of tax exempt funds has neither been thoroughly studied nor convincingly demonstrated.[9]

As for the public sector, the report of the Task Force on State Regulation of Charitable Organizations of the Commission on Private Philanthropy and Public Needs has this to say:

A majority of the states do practically nothing in fulfilling their obligation to the public of safeguarding the billions of dollars controlled by charitable trusts and foundations in this country.[10]

Note was taken in the report of the fact that many Attorneys General were woefully understaffed to carry out a regulatory function, that relatively few states employ accountants to examine financial data when received, that only thirteen states require registration, and that only fifteen states require annual reporting. The situation is somewhat different in respect to state regulation of charitable soliticitations. A total of thirty-one states have enacted charitable solicitation statutes. Apart from the staffing problem, many of these states have split the functions of registration, usually in the hands of the Secretary of State, and enforcement, under the aegis of the Attorney

General, thus leaving the door open to bureaucratic delays. As the report says, "Since the professional fund raiser has the ability to move between states with relative ease, time delays can become one of the most harmful elements blocking effective legislation."[11]

One may well ask, where can we go from here? It has helped us to formulate what we see the purposes of regulation to be. At risk of oversimplification there are three:

1. To protect the public generally, and contributors particularly, from fraud and misrepresentation.
2. To assure that funds spent are done so consistent with corporate purpose and applicable laws.
3. To help organizations to do a better job, thus assuring, among other things, public confidence and support.

The first purpose of regulation—to protect the public, particularly contributors—represents the operation of the police powers of government to control the conduct of its citizens in the interest of welfare, safety, or health of the people. As the Supreme Court held in the case of *Cantwell v. Connecticut,* 310 U.S. 296 (1940):

> Without doubt a State may protect its citizens from fraudulent soliticitation by requiring a stranger in the community, before permitting him publicly to solicit funds for any purpose, to establish his identity and his authority to act for the cause which he purports to represent. The State

> is likewise free to regulate the time and manner
> of solicitation generally, in the interest of public
> safety, peace, comfort or convenience.

The courts have also held that this governmental power may extend to regulating the cost of charitable solicitation. (*National Foundation v. City of Fort Worth*, 415 F 2nd 41 (5th Circuit, 1969).) However, the courts have also held that solicitation of funds for worthy charitable organizations comes within the Constitutional guarantees of freedom of speech, freedom of the press and liberty of action, and that regulation of charitable solicitation is subject to Constitutional standards of equal protection of laws, and due process. (*American Cancer Society v. City of Dayton*, 114 N.D. 2nd 219, 224 (Ohio, 1953))

A Model Bill on this subject, drafted by a committee of the National Health Council, affords a vehicle around which all can rally. John J. O'Connor, Special Counsel to the National Foundation, who drafted the Model Bill, sees the following objectives to be served by such legislation:

1. To prevent the contributing public from being victimized by charlatans and unethical organizations and individuals.

2. To keep the contributing public, at all times, fully informed concerning the programs, purposes, methods of solicitation, solicitation costs and administrative costs of organizations and individuals seeking charitable contributions from the general public.

3. To insure the enactment of legislation that will not contain capricious, arbitrary, unreasonable, and punitive restrictions upon the

legitimate activities and programs of accredited agencies and reputable professional fundraising counsel and professional solicitors.

4. To enable a state official (Secretary of State or Attorney General) to require a full disclosure of programs, methods of solicitation, solicitation costs and administrative costs of all individuals and organizations soliciting contributions in the state; and to empower such official to temporarily or permanently prevent public solicitations by any individual or organization not complying in all respects with the registration and reporting requirements.

5. To eventually lead to a uniform law on this subject, thereby hopefully substantially reducing for the administrative agencies of the various states, the charitable organizations having branches, affiliates or chapters therein and professional fund-raising counsel and professional solicitors doing business therein the amount of time and expense presently spent in connection with the enforcement of and compliance with numerous laws of this nature, both at the state and local level, which vary considerably in applicability and content.[12]

The two concepts which appeal greatly to us are uniformity and reciprocity. They symbolize, in a way, the essential conflict in regulatory activity which we mentioned at the beginning of this chapter, i.e., between the rights of the state or the public, on the one hand, and the rights of the individual or organization on the other. In this case the interests of the state and of the organization could both be served by uniformity and reciprocity. Consider that a theoretical state-wide child care organization in New York now has to go through the following processes in order to operate: incorporation, licensing, reporting to the State Department of Social Services annually, reporting to the IRS annually, reporting, if requested, to the Philanthropic Advisory Department of the Council of Better Business Bureaus, the National Information Bureau, and local United Ways in the state from which the organization may seek funds. Is it any wonder that the reputable organizations have some resistance to further regulation? The importance of provision for reciprocal agreements, especially as it involves national organizations with local affiliates, is substantial. A section on the Model Law makes provision for the appropriate official of the state to accept information filed in another state or with the IRS if such information is "substantially similar to the information required under this act." This same provision is also made applicable to organizations organized under the laws of another state having their principal place of business outside the state and whose funds are derived principally from sources outside the state, i.e., national organizations whose local affiliate(s) are within the scope of the Model Act.

There remain two complex issues, however. The first: Should such an act contain a specific fund-raising limitation? There appear to be three alternatives. One alternative is to establish a limit of, say, 35 percent, which is uniform and clearly understandable. On the other hand, a figure of 30 percent may be high for a particular organization at a particular time. Moreover, as Jack Grimes points out in his report to the Commission on Private Philanthropy and Public Needs entitled *"The Fund-Raising Percent as a Quantitative Standard for Regulation of Public Charities,"*

> the fund-raising cost percentage as a standard can provide, at best, an approximation of agency efficiency in raising money for a specified time period, but it cannot measure the agency's effectiveness in meeting needs. . . . There are causative factors unrelated to abuse or fraud for variations in fund-raising cost percentages among charitable organizations and for the same organization for different time periods.[13]

A second alternative, as used in the Model Act, is to utilize a "reasonable percent," thus freeing the responsible state official to determine each organization's status on a case-by-case basis, taking into account all of the circumstances. A third possible alternative is to utilize a fixed formula, but to place the onus on the state official to initiate action if it were felt that the expenditures were improper, even though within the formula, with the burden of proof on the organization, if the percent of funds exceeded the fixed amount. On the basis of our present knowledge we would prefer the "reasonable percent" approach.

The second complex issue is whether religious organizations and religiously affiliated organizations should be brought within the scope of the act, particularly when such organizations, while nominally controlled by bona fide religious groups, may be engaged in activities which are not primarily religious. The Model Law makes a distinction between "religious purposes" and "secular" activities in the definitions section and requires that religious organizations register with respect to the latter.

In so doing the drafters followed the example of the court in *Gospel Army v. Los Angeles* 27 Cal. 232, appeal dismissed 331 U.S. 453 (1947), in which the Court notes that where the public solicitation by religious organizations or their affiliates is not solely for the preservation or advancement of religion, the state may regulate that part of the solicitation which benefits a charitable rather than a religious purpose. The state (as well as the church) has an interest in the welfare of its citizens apart from any religious connotations, although many regard the practice of charity as a religious duty.

The second purpose of regulation—assurance that the funds of a charitable organization are spent in accordance with the approved purpose of the charity and that trustees are properly carrying out their fiduciary responsibilities—derives both from common and statutory law. Because of the way in which charities have evolved in the United States it is a responsibility vested in both state and federal law.

With respect to state responsibility the record, as we have seen, is uneven. However, as a goal (possibly just an ideal) we would like to see all the states adopt, as a basis for an effective program of regulation, "The Uniform Supervision of Trustees for Charitable Purposes Act" as modified in the report of the Ad Hoc Task Force report to the Commission on Private Philanthropy and Public Needs. Such a development would go far toward establishing a more unified body of charitable law, which now, as Marion Fremont-Smith has observed, draws more on trust and corporate law.[14]

It would also serve to correct the abuses reported by the Ohio Attorney General in the course of his survey of the status of state regulation of charitable trusts, foundations, and solicitations.[15] Eighteen states reported that the most frequently encountered abuses were: 1) excessive fees, related to trustee compensation as well as professional fund-raising charges in connection with a charitable solicitation; 2) self-dealing, entailing improper conduct in which the trustee personally benefits from his position of trust; and 3) the failure to correspond, register, or report, thus preventing accessibility to information and making effective regulation difficult.

The practical and positive effect, were all states to enact the Uniform Law, would, of course, be uniformity. Uniformity in accounting and reporting procedures would go a long way toward easing the present burdens of reporting. The Tax Reform Act of 1969 made it mandatory upon private foundations to file copies of Form 990 with the appropriate state enforcement agency. It is desirable that this requirement be extended to all charities, and that there be a free exchange of information between the IRS and state regulatory agencies.

We do not have a firm judgment on what would be the optimum distribution of responsibility for regulation at the federal level. We think the subject needs greater debate before firm opinions are adopted. The basic issue, which has emerged in current dialogue, is whether there should be a national commission of some kind and, if so, what its relationship to the Internal Revenue Service should be. It should be recalled that there have been two major efforts, neither of which bore fruit, to establish a national commission on philanthropy. The first took place in 1963 as a follow-up of the Exploratory Study by an Ad Hoc Committee, the 1961 report of which was entitled *Voluntary Health and Welfare Agencies in the United States.* The proposal was for creating a National Committee on Voluntary Health and Welfare Agencies, and its general purposes were defined as follows:

> . . . to encourage increased participation of the American people in voluntary health and welfare

> organizations; to foster more effective operations
> and programs under voluntary auspices; to
> strengthen the leadership of such agencies and
> extend and deepen the influence of the entire
> voluntary effort in the nation.[16]

This effort never came to fruition, even though it deliberately excluded any regulatory function from its purposes. This effort was followed by a recommendation of the Commission on Foundations and Private Philanthropy in 1969 that there be an Advisory Board of Philanthropic Policy.[17] The Board was to be composed of from ten to fifteen "outstanding private citizens selected from the leadership segments of society that are concerned with social and philanthropic programs—public and private."[18] The Committee expressed a preference for presidential appointment and Senate confirmation. The Board was to be a continuing body, with overlapping terms, to be concerned with philanthropy as a whole, and would have the power to obtain information from private organizations and state and federal agencies. An agenda was not suggested but it was assumed that the Board might undertake the following:

1. Providing information to Congress, the President, and the public on the needs and state of philanthropy and charitable organizations.
2. Continuing evaluation of the regulation of charitable organizations, particularly the work of the Internal Revenue Service.
3. Continuing review of the effectiveness and current operation of the tax incentive system.

What the Commission saw as necessary was a long-range reassessment of basic tax and regulatory policy affecting philanthropic giving and charitable organizations. Like the recommendation of the earlier group, this recommendation never got off the ground.

It is our view that the functions of the Internal Revenue Service and the functions which may be sought through federal regulation are incongruous, despite the creation via the Pension Act in 1974 of the position of Assistant Commissioner of Internal Revenue for Employee Benefit Plans and Exempt Organizations. Even here the title is bifurcated so that primary concern is not with "exempt organizations"! Essentially the job and the orientation of the IRS is the collection of taxes, a mammoth task, and not the strengthening of the voluntary sector. In an article "Public Supervision of Philanthropy and Charity—Can It Be Improved?" Sheldon Cohen, a former Commissioner of Internal Revenue, is quoted as follows:

> The way to get ahead in the Internal Revenue Service, obviously, is to do the thing that is most important to the Internal Revenue Service. And that thing is collecting taxes. And that thing is not granting exemptions. So that the agents who work these cases in the field. . . . get brownie points not for granting exemptions but for denying them. And therefore their tendency is not to be helpful but to be harmful. And this is not in criticism of any individual or of any individual action, or indeed the organizational structure. They're doing the best they know how.[19]

One is inclined to contrast this adversary kind of relationship with that of the British Charity Commission which proceeds in its various functions of advice, supervision, and regulation on the assumption that the aims of individual trustees are the same as those of the Commissioners, namely, the improvement of the administration of charity.[20]

Others have been critical of the Internal Revenue Service because of its lack of vigorous and effective enforcement of the laws governing exempt organizations. For example, the IRS is reluctant to rule in advance, with respect to the conformity of prospective actions, again preferring to take an adversary posture after the fact.[21] One is left to speculate whether continuous review of possible abuses, together with close cooperation with state regulatory agencies where these exist, might have had the effect of increasing public confidence, thus reducing to some extent the cyclical concerns which have arisen since the Second World War.

We think there are two principal options for change at this time. The first option would be to transfer certain functions from the Internal Revenue Service to a national center for the supervision of charitable trusts. The testimony of Alan Pifer, President of the Carnegie Corporation, before the Subcommittee on Foundations of the Senate Committee on Finance, in October 1973, spells out the possible functions of such a center:

1. The center would have the power to determine what is charitable and to grant or deny tax exemption accordingly, although this power might be limited by a right of appeal to the courts.

2. The center would maintain a publicly available register. Listing in this register would be an organization's guarantee that it enjoyed tax exempt, charitable status.

3. The center would conduct audits of the opera-

tion of tax exempt, charitable organizations.

4. The center would have the duty to see to it that the legal standards applying to charity were enforced.

5. The center would, when requested, give advisory opinions with respect to the legal consequences of proposed actions by charitable organizations.

6. The center would gather data about all aspects of charity, would issue publications periodically, and would provide information to the public on request.[22]

Pifer goes on to note that such a center should be concerned only with charity; it should rest on the assumption that charity exists for the benefit of the community and that the essential purpose of supervision is affirmative—to protect, strengthen, and encourage charity and to build public confidence in it; and it should recognize that the states have basic powers and responsibilities in respect to charity and that it would be the center's duty to develop means of cooperation in furtherance of joint federal and state objectives.

The second option is, as we see it, to leave the present functions of the Internal Revenue Service intact, and to develop on the national level a commission which would have functions modeled after the Advisory Commission on Intergovernmental Relations. That Commission is a permanent independent body established by federal, state, and local governments. It meets four times a year, reviews the important issues or problems which have arisen in interrelationships between federal, state, and local governments and assigns certain of these issues to staff for study. Following study, the Commission then votes upon the study and the recommendations, and having taken this action, then undertakes to publicize and persuade the various levels of government to adopt their recommendations. It has no regulatory function, and no powers beyond the study and implementation role as described.

There is, of course, a third option—to leave matters exactly as they are; but we feel that the times and needs of the field require change. If we were required to vote on this last issue, we would vote today for Pifer's formulation, admittedly an ideal proposal. Why, in this field of regulation, do we pursue the ideal, rather than trying to find a compromise? For the simple reason that, in our view, individual organizations and the general public will benefit most from attainment of the ideal. Again there are options. Some may feel that regulation should just go away, but we think this is unrealistic. Or we can go on as we are for another decade or two, until the ideal is reached. One reason we urge that the ideal state of affairs be hastened by all possible means is that any shortfall simply compounds the present patchwork design and produces confusion, overlapping, and incredible burdens on organizations to conform. Meanwhile the public is similarly confused, suspicious, and untrusting. The only solution is to get from "here to there" as quickly as possible whether a compromise or the ideal.

The third purpose of regulation, according to our simplified formula, is to help organizations to do a better job, thus assuring, among other things, public confidence and support. It is in this area that we see self-regulation having its major role. As Meek observes, the objective of self-regulation is to meet recognized standards. Once developed, standards are publicized, disseminated, and utilized by agencies to improve administration and services. They ultimately are used in processes of accreditation.[23]

Typically, Meek says, standards reflect contemporary research and professional judgment (best practice) and are concerned with requisite characteristics (inputs), service delivery (process), and results obtained (outputs). This conceptualization is extremely useful, in part because it tends to place primary emphasis on service, although not to the neglect of other components, and because it suggests one reason for the frustration of many persons at the limitation of cost-benefit data for many organizations. They simply do not have techniques for measuring outputs, except in quantitative terms! However, more consideration of that problem will appear in a later chapter.

Nor have we any factual basis for disagreeing with Meek's conclusion that, when measured by criteria of coverage of all voluntary organizations, self-regulation has touched primarily the established organizations in the fields of education, health, and welfare. When the full history of self-regulation is written it will doubtless be recorded that self-regulation is more successful when it is attached to some objective that is seen as important: accreditation by the Joint Committee on Accreditation of Hospitals is important because only then is the hospital eligible for Hill-Burton money; accreditation by the Child Welfare League of America is important because only then can the local child care agency continue membership in this prestigious organization; a "clean bill of health" by the National Information Bureau is important in order for the organization to receive a corporate grant; accreditation is important because the more qualified professionals prefer to work only in accredited agencies. A great deal of experience and some research has suggested that organizations tend to make more improvements when there is some external force, pressure, or rationale than under other circumstances. This should not be a surprising conclusion because many organizations tend to become, in varying degrees, institutionalized and resistant to change.

The experience of organizations within the health and welfare field is instructive. The development of revised standards of accounting is one example of self-regulation at its best, even though this view is doubtless not enthusiastically embraced by all national voluntary organizations within that very field. The Ad Hoc Committee's report in 1961 has the following to say about public reporting:

> Voluntary agencies derive their support primarily from the public and have a duty to the public to disclose fully those activities that do not involve confidential relationships with clients. Failure to give accurate and complete information is a breach of the agency's fiduciary responsibility to its supporting public. The public as the investor in an agency has the right to know the facts. The agency as the recipient of public funds has the duty to disclose fully to those who invest in its activities.
>
> This duty of full disclosure has not been carried out by some agencies. A few have even unjustifiably denied this obligation. Others have provided misleading information.[24]

A major recommendation of the report was that there be developed a system of uniform accounting and financial reporting for voluntary agencies.

The response to this mandate, as it was correctly interpreted by leaders in the health and welfare field, was the formation of a Joint Liaison Committee by the National Health Council and the National Social Welfare Assembly and the publication in 1964 of the *Standards of*

Accounting and Financial Reporting for Voluntary Health and Welfare Organizations. [25]

For the next three years the sponsoring organizations engaged in a program of implementation among their constituents, an effort primarily funded by several foundations. Compliance with the standards was made a condition of membership with the National Health Council, but was on a voluntary basis for those organizations associated with the National Social Welfare Assembly. Adoption of the standards was uneven among NSWA agencies, and the reluctance of some organizations was abetted by the fact that the American Institute of Certified Public Accountants, the standard-setting organization for the accounting industry, adopted an *Audit Guide* in 1966 for accountants performing audits for voluntary health and welfare organizations which did not endorse the standards and contained several significant deviations from them. [26]

The situation was further complicated by the fact that there was no central body to which organizations could turn for interpretation of the standards, and thus they came into serious danger of being eroded by exception. (A National Social Welfare Assembly-National Health Council proposal to create a Center for the Promotion of Uniform Accounting Standards, over a period of five years, could not be funded.)

In an effort to deal with these and other questions a new Liaison Committee was formed in 1972 consisting of representatives of NSWA (now the National Assembly for Social Policy and Development), the National Health Council, and the United Way of America. Almost simultaneously, the American Institute of Certified Public Accountants formed a new Committee on Voluntary Health and Welfare Organizations, and the two groups began a series of joint meetings. An outcome of these meetings was resolution of the major issues that had differentiated the earlier industry *Audit Guide* from the standards, and the publication, in September 1973 of an *Industry Audit Guide,* for Audits of Voluntary Health and Welfare Organizations, and the revision of the standards in the fall of 1974 in order to achieve conformity. The preface to the Industry Audit Guide contains the statement, "This revised audit guide describes generally accepted accounting principles applicable to financial reporting by health and welfare organizations."[27] Because a period of adaptation was necessary the Industry Audit Guide was to be required for fiscal years beginning July 1, 1975.

Thus, by 1974 the health and welfare sector had achieved a major milestone in self-regulation. Not only were the standards acceptable to the voluntary health and welfare fields and the accounting industry, they even were endorsed by the United States Civil Service Commission in its administration of the Combined Federal Campaign Plan, they were incorporated into the regulations of several state and local regulatory agencies, and used by the U.S. Department of Health, Education and Welfare for developing indirect cost rates for voluntary health and welfare agencies receiving grants and contracts.

It is submitted that this is a prodigious record of achievement in self-regulation over a period of approximately ten years. In retrospect, it is difficult to account for the reluctance of a few national organizations to embrace enthusiastically the standards. Conformity a decade ago by all organizations might have reduced later demands for excessive regulation arising from public disclosure of a few cases of excessive fund-raising or administrative costs. The principal thrust of the standards for full disclosure, and for differentiating and breaking out the costs of fund raising, program services, and management costs can only serve to enhance the credibility, public confidence, and support for all agencies, and work to the benefit of voluntarism as a whole. One is forced to conclude that some organizations see their responsibility for accountability ending with their own constituencies, rather than with the public at large.

Beyond this classic example of self-regulation the major organizations within the health and welfare field are blanketed by several review, self-regulatory, and accreditation processes. Two effective operations that fall between "pure" self-regulation and government regulation are the National Information Bureau and the Philanthropic Advisory Department of the Council of Better Business Bureaus. Founded in 1882 as the Contributors' Information Bureau of the Charity Organization Society of New York City, the National Information Bureau was created in 1920 in an effort to bring some order out of the proliferation of wartime and post-war appeals. Since that time NIB has grown in scope and reputation, particularly as it became a valuable aid to growing corporate philanthropy. Today, its purpose is two-fold: to maintain sound standards in the field of philanthropy; and to aid wise giving through its confidential reports and advisory services for contributors. During 1972 NIB distributed about 25,700 of its confidential reports on some 400 to 500 agencies to its membership of corporations, foundations, individuals, Chambers of Commerce, Better Business Bureaus, governmental agencies, and local United Ways, national health and welfare organizations, and so forth. It is important to note that the character of the report is both factual and evaluative, and compliance with the following basic standards is considered essential for NIB approval:

1. Board—an active and responsible governing body, serving without compensation, holding regular meetings, and with effective administrative control.

2. Purpose—a legitimate purpose with no avoidable duplication of the work of other sound organizations.

3. Program—reasonable efficiency in program management and reasonable adequacy of resources, both material and personnel.

4. Cooperation—evidence of consultation and cooperation with established agencies in the same or related fields.

5. Ethical promotion—ethical methods of publicity, promotion, and solicitation of funds.

6. Fund-raising practices—a) no payment of commissions for fund-raising, b) no mailing of unordered tickets or merchandise with a request for money in return, c) no general telephone solicitation of the public.

7. Audit—an annual audit, preferably employing the Uniform Accounting Standards and prepared by an independent certified public accountant, showing all support/revenue and expenditures in reasonable detail. New organizations should provide an independent certified accountant's statement that a proper financial system has been installed.

8. Detailed annual budget—translating program plan into financial terms.[28]

The Council of Better Business Bureaus has recently formulated standards to be applied to soliciting organizations in respect to which the Philanthropic Advisory Department makes reports. The foreword to the *Standards for Charitable Solicitations* contains the following:

> To encourage public support of reputable philanthropic endeavors and to advance high standards of ethical conduct among all soliciting organizations, the Better Business Bureaus have developed these basic standards relating to the structure, finances, fund-raising methods, and the advertising and informational materials of such organizations. They are not intended to restrict charitable solicitations but are issued in the belief that both the general public and soliciting organizations will benefit by full and accurate disclosure of all information which potential donors may need and reasonably wish to consider in a decision on where their help is needed and how well their contributions of time and money will be utilized.[29]

The reports of the CBBB are available free of charge to all inquirers, and are automatically sent to the 150 Better Business Bureaus, over 700 Chambers of Commerce, as well as the CBBB business members. The Philanthropic Advisory Department maintains files on over 5,000 soliciting organizations.

Both the NIB and the CBBB, by the application of their standards, are helping organizations to regulate themselves. But of course self-regulation goes much further than these important efforts. Individual organizations, through the development of standards and accreditation processes, have an important impact on the structure, operations, and quality of services of their affiliated organizations. The United Way of America administers a program for its affiliates identified as *Standards of Excellence for Local United Way Organizations.* Such organizations as the Child Welfare League of America, the Family Service Association of America, the American Heart Association, the National Easter Seal Society for Crippled Children and Adults, the National League for Nursing, and the National Council for Homemaker-Home Health Aide Services all operate programs for their affiliates through which attainment and maintenance of standards are sought.

Brief mention should be made of the membership standards for voluntary health organizations of the National Health Council achieved through the Participating Agency Review program, consisting of the completion of a detailed questionnaire and on-site peer visits. The National Accreditation Council for Agencies Serving the Blind and Visually Handicapped applies a comprehensive set of standards to all aspects of the operations of agencies being reviewed. The work of the Joint Commission on Accreditation of Hospitals is familiar to many, and its program now includes long-term care facilities (nursing homes and homes for the aged), psychiatric facilities (public and private psychiatric hospitals, community mental health centers, psychiatric outpatient clinics, children's psychiatric facilities and partial hospitalization programs), and facilities and agencies providing service to mentally retarded and other developmentally disabled persons. The guidelines recently issued by the Department of Health, Education and Welfare for the new Professional Standards Review Organizations state that where such an organization delegates the medical care evaluation study requirements to a hospital, Joint Commission accreditation of that hospital is satisfactory fulfillment of the requirement.

We have spent so much time on the subject of regulation because we think it raises important questions which will be before the general public in the next few years, and that the future vitality of the voluntary sector depends upon how these issues are resolved. We advance our own conclusions with some trepidation—because no one really has the final or best answer. Returning to our formulation of the purposes of regulation, we think that the first of these—protection of the public generally, and contributors particularly, from fraud and misrepresentation—is a public function that belongs at the state level. The second purpose—to assure that funds spent are done so consistent with corporate purpose and applicable laws —is similarly a public function, but in this case it is necessarily shared between the states and the federal government. The third and final purpose—to help organizations to do a better job, thus assuring, among other things, public confidence and support—is, we believe, a purpose best pursued by the voluntary sector through the mechanism of self-regulation. At this time we think that the major thrust should be in the direction of establishing equitable and uniform state and federal legislation. Only then will it be possible to break out of the maze of confusion which presently surrounds the whole field of regulation, and establish a firm basis upon which the voluntary sector can develop its own standards.

Another way of looking at regulation is to postulate that public responsibility is essentially the exercise of the police power of the state to protect the consumer and the general public from fraud, misrepresentation, and the occasional venality of human beings. The voluntary organization's role, on the other hand, is to develop higher standards of performance consonant with its own goals and objectives. To the extent that the voluntary sector can maintain ever more effective, rigorous, and more widely accepted and applied standards, to that extent it will foreclose the extension of public control into those areas. The Tax Reform Act of 1969 codified a set of standards for private foundations, which the foundations could not do for themselves, in part because of the great diversity within their constituency. However, that problem did not impede the heavy hand of public regulation with effects we have described earlier. Among the lessons to be learned from that experience is that a voluntary organization's accountability must always be reckoned, not only in terms of its "usual" constituencies of board, members, persons it serves, sources of funds, and so on, but also in terms of the general public.

NOTES

1. CHARLES SAMPSON, Memorandum to the 501 (c) (3) Group from the Chairman, November 1, 1974, p. 1. (Mimeographed.)
2. NORRIS E. CLASS, "The Regulatory Challenge to Social Work: An Historical Essay on Professional Policy Formulation" (Paper written for the National Association of Social Workers, Washington, D.C., January 1, 1973), p. 3.
3. HENRY C. SUHRKE, ed., "State Regulation," *The Philanthropy Monthly*, 7 (December, 1974), p. 22.
4. Ibid., p. 23.
5. HENRY C. SUHRKE, ed., "The Impact of the Minimum Distribution Rule on Foundations," *Non-Profit Report*, 6 (March 1974), p. 15.
6. Ibid., p. 20.
7. HENRY C. SUHRKE, ed., "Foundation Giving: The Outlook for 1975," *The Philanthropy Monthly*, 7 (November 1974), p. 13.
8. United Way of America, "Mondale Introduces 'Truth in Contributions' Act," *Focus on Federal Relations*, June 16, 1975, p. 2.
9. PETER G. MEEK, Consultant, "Self-Regulation in Private Philanthropy" (Report prepared for the Commission on Private Philanthropy and Public Needs, September 1974), p. 181. The findings and conclusions here, related to this report, are those of the present authors only and not of the Commission.
10. HENRY C. SUHRKE, ed., "State Regulation," *The Philanthropy Monthly*, 7 (December 1974), p. 23.
11. Ibid., p. 25.
12. HENRY C. SUHRKE, "An Editor's Note," *Non-Profit Report*, 6 (November 1973), p. 14.
13. ARTHUR J. GRIMES, "The Fund-Raising Percent as a

Quantitative Standard for Regulation of Public Charities"
(Report to the Commission on Private Philanthropy and
Public Needs, March 1975), p. 4. See comment at note 9,
above.

14. MARION FREMONT-SMITH, quoted in "The Status of State
Regulation of the Charitable Trusts, Foundations, and
Solicitations. (Report of the Attorney General to the Commission on Private Philanthropy and Public Needs, March
1975), p. 3. See comment at note 9, above.

15. Ohio Attorney General's Office, "The Status of State Regulation of Charitable Trusts, Foundations and Solicitations"
(Report to the Commission on Private Philanthropy and
Public Needs, December 28, 1974), p. 142. See comment at
note 9, above.

16. Ohio Attorney General's Office, ibid., p. 67.

17. PETER G. MEEK, Consultant, op. cit., p. 45.

18. Commission on Foundations and Private Philanthropy, Peter G. Peterson, Chairman, *Foundations, Private Giving,
and Public Policy* (Chicago: University of Chicago Press,
1970), p. 181.

19. SHELDON COHEN, "Private Supervision of Philanthropy
and Charity, Can It Be Improved?" *Non-Profit Report,* 6
(December 1973), p. 16.

20. MARION FREMONT-SMITH, "Public Supervision of Philanthropy and Charity, Can It Be Improved?" *Non-Profit Report,* 6 (December 1973), p. 23.

21. THOMAS TROYER, "Public Supervision of Philanthropy
and Charity, Can It Be Improved?" *Non-Profit Report,* 6
(December 1973), p. 21.

22. Ohio Attorney General's Office, op. cit., p. 54.

23. PETER G. MEEK, Consultant, op. cit., p. 5.

24. Ad Hoc Citizens Committee, *Voluntary Health and Welfare Agencies in the United States* (New York: The Schoolmasters' Press, 1961), p. 11.

25. *Standards of Accounting and Financial Reporting for Voluntary Health and Welfare Organizations* (New York: Na-

tional Health Council, National Social Welfare Assembly, 1964).

26. Committee on Voluntary Health and Welfare Organizations, *Audits of Voluntary Health and Welfare Organizations* (New York: American Institute of Certified Public Accountants, 1966), p. 1.

27. Committee on Voluntary Health and Welfare Organizations, *Industry Audit Guide, Audits of Voluntary Health and Welfare Organizations* (New York: American Institute of Certified Public Accountants, 1974), p. vi.

28. National Information Bureau, "Basic Standards in Philanthropy" (New York: The National Assembly for Social Policy and Development, 1973), p. 6. (Mimeographed.)

29. Better Business Bureau, *Standards for Charitable Solicitations* (Washington, D.C.: Council of Better Business Bureaus, Inc. 1974), p. iii.

5 TAX REFORM

A MAJOR THREAT to voluntarism over the past decade or so, most serious because of its persistence, has been the prospective impact of tax reform proposals on the charitable contribution deduction. One would expect that voluntary organizations, depending in varying degrees as they do upon the tax deductible contributions of individuals, would be the beneficiaries of tax policies reflecting the consistent and affirmative support which the federal government has historically accorded voluntary effort. Regrettably, this is not the case. Instead, voluntary organizations within the whole spectrum of philanthropy, including education, hospitals, health services, social welfare, the arts, environment and civic groups, are, as a result of proposals for tax reform, repeatedly forced into defensive postures from which they have had to battle for their very existence.

Why is this so, and from whence have the attacks come? In the main, from two sources. The first is a small but distinguished group of tax experts and economists who adhere to the "tax expenditure" theory; the second group is composed of those individuals who perceive voluntary effort as an elitist enterprise, created and controlled by a few persons of wealth.

Taxable expenditure is a term fostered by Stanley Surrey, its foremost advocate, to define

> revenue losses attributable to a special exclusion,
> exemption, or deduction from gross income or to
> a special credit, preferential rate of tax, or defer-

ral of tax liability. Tax expenditures are one
means by which public policy objectives are pursued by the Federal Government and, in most
cases, can be viewed as alternatives to budget
outlays, credit assistance, or other instruments of
public policy.[1]

Among the fifty-one so-called tax expenditure items in the
1976 federal budget the imputed expenditure for individual charitable contributions is in the amount of $4.9 billion.

In our view there are at least two aspects of the tax
expenditure concept which are intrinsically wrong. The
first is that it places undue emphasis upon the revenue
impact of the charitable gift. We have yet to read anything
written by an advocate of the tax expenditure theory
which goes beyond the revenue supposedly "lost" by the
federal government to a serious consideration of what
contributed dollars actually finance—namely, support of
programs and services provided to people by the various
organizations, which programs and services otherwise
would or should be provided by government. This line of
reasoning is deficient in that it emphasizes economic
rather than social aspects of tax policy.

It is interesting to note that the then newly enacted personal income tax law was amended in 1917 to
authorize the charitable contribution deduction when tax
rates were sharply increased to finance the war. The enactment of the deduction was intended to prevent the higher
tax rates from substantially reducing philanthropy. In
other words, contribution deductibility was added to the
tax law not so much to create an incentive for giving as
to avoid interfering with the preexisting relationship between donors and the organizations of their choice. It was

the system of voluntarism which the drafters of the early tax laws were attempting to preserve.[2]

The second problem with the tax expenditure theory is that it regards the charitable contribution as, in effect, a subsidy and thus implies a measure of potential control and accountability that otherwise would not be present. This is not necessarily bad. For example, voluntary agencies which are direct recipients of federal money are required to adopt affirmative action plans establishing goals for the hiring of women and members of minority groups. Certainly it would be desirable for all voluntary organizations to take such a step. This same line of reasoning might well lead to broader community representation on the governing board of an organization, a subject which will be discussed elsewhere in this book. But the essential problem remains one of degree of control. As we have indicated in the previous chapter various proposals are under consideration for the federal government to regulate the solicitations and expenditures of voluntary agencies and organizations. To what extent will acceptance of the validity of the subsidy concept make these regulatory provisions more onerous than they need to be or otherwise would have been?

Proponents of the contribution "subsidy" system would indeed do away with the present system of contribution deductibility, but they would not permit voluntary organizations to perish. Instead, they would establish a system of matching grants by which all individuals' gifts to voluntary organizations would be matched by direct federal grants. The individual would make his nondeductible contribution, compute the federal matching percentage, and designate the organization or organizations to which the federal matching funds should be paid. In our view the predictable outcomes of such a matching grant system would be a reduction in institutional independence and donor privacy, and a reduction in the incentive to make charitable gifts since they no longer would generate tax benefits for the donor. An even more serious problem is that a matching grant system could not be set up to accommodate the constitutional problems of churches and church-related activities. A matching grant system which applied to nonsectarian agencies and a contribution deduction system which applied to churches and church-related agencies would differentiate between such categories in a way which would discriminate seriously against the former. In addition, it would further complicate tax law administration.

In a 1971 speech summarizing the matching grant idea, Boris Bittker made a profound analysis of the impact of such a system on voluntary organizations.[3] He notes at once that it would not be possible to enact a system of matching grants that included churches, and doubts the feasibility of a system of matching grants made to secular agencies, with, at the same time, a perpetuation of tax deductions for contributions made to churches. He then goes on to assert that matching grants would not be the functional equivalent of tax deductions in the pattern of benefits conferred on charitable institutions. He comments:

> It would be difficult to devise a formula for matching grants that would produce, even in the aggregate, the same amount of revenue that charities owe to the tax deduction, and it is almost inconceivable that this could be done for particular charities or even categories of charities.[4]

Bittker concludes his consideration of matching grants by asserting that they would not produce the donor and institutional independence that now is accepted by the Internal Revenue Code and by the Internal Revenue Service's administration of relevant provisions:

> Acknowledging that a dogmatic conclusion is not warranted, I must say that I have very little confidence that a system of matching grants would be administered without administrative and congressional investigations, loyalty oaths, informal or implicit warnings against heterodoxy, and other trappings of governmental support that the tax deduction has, so far, been able to escape.[5]

In our judgment this analysis of the matching grant system exposes the ultimate flaw in the position of those who advocate adoption of the tax expenditure concept—that they have no viable alternative to the present system. The issue is thus joined. The only alternative to a pluralistic system of organizations, services and activities is a monolithic condition in which either government does it all, or, at the least, controls how it is to be done. Most Americans, we believe, would reject this option if confronted with the choice. The principle that government should allow a portion of its revenues to be diverted to achieve this pluralism through the mechanism of contributions deductibility has been consistently embraced by the American people and their elected representatives. Nothing that has happened in recent years could justify a departure from this principle. Indeed, the need for its application has increased.

If carried to its logical conclusion (elimination of

the charitable deduction and the substitution of government grants) there could be only one possible outcome: a few small private agencies supported by nondeductible contributions and other sources of revenue, such as fees and income from endowments, with the vast majority of those remaining falling under the control of government through a system of matching grants or subsidies.

The belief that voluntary organizations are bastions of the elite arises from a number of erroneous assumptions and misconceptions. While it may have been true at one time, it no longer is true that a few persons of wealth control or dominate the voluntary sector by their gifts. Of total giving of $24.5 billion in 1973, only $232 million, or .009 percent, constituted gifts of a million dollars or more made by individual donors. Moreover, 67.2 percent of these large gifts were concentrated in the areas of the arts and the humanities as well as being made to institutions of higher learning, many of them probably earmarked for capital construction. The average aggregate gifts made by individuals to philanthropy in 1972 was $490, with the average for individuals with adjusted gross incomes of $100,000 or more equaling $13,444. Gifts to United Way organizations, important to the field of social welfare although small in relation to total giving, are derived from three basic sources in the following approximate percentages: corporate gifts, 30–35 percent; payroll deductions, 60–65 percent; and executive or large individual gifts, 5 percent. This suggests that the majority of United Way gifts are received from persons in the middle-income brackets. This is not to say that the role of the big giver is not important. Experienced fund raisers know that the large gift is sought early in any campaign as a pace setter, as a standard for others to emulate, and as a psychological stimulus for the entire campaign.

Another assumption of those advocating greater

public control is that governmental budgeting processes are efficient, and that voluntary allocation processes are inefficient and dominated by special interests. Our experience leads us to vigorous rejection of this erroneous conclusion. Based upon the successes achieved in matching resources to needs, it is our conclusion that the budgeting processes of most United Way and Jewish Federation allocations committees are equally, if not more effective than their public counterparts, which all too frequently are characterized by political pressure-response syndromes and by political trade-offs.

Many voluntary organizations have been held suspect in the matter of full financial disclosure, even though the development in the health and welfare fields of uniform standards of accounting and reporting has made it possible for voluntary agencies using these standards to achieve, justifiably, a fuller measure of public credibility and confidence.

One additional assumption made by those who claim that voluntary organizations are elitist—that agency boards have a narrow, exclusive composition—must be challenged. We will discuss this concept in depth elsewhere, but suffice it to say that the goal of wider participation in agency governance has radically changed the patterns of board and committee membership in many agencies and organizations. Affirmative action programs have had a salutary effect. From the concept of "maximum feasible participation of persons served," which originated in the antipoverty programs of the 1960s, has come general acceptance of the idea that people have a right to participate in those decisions which affect them. And although the results may not be as egalitarian as some would have it, the idea has taken deep root as an important value within the voluntary sector.

Of course, the argument made by those who identify the voluntary sector with elitism is carried over into the area of tax reform, where issues of equity are raised. For example, the "cost" of a gift of $1,000 to a person in the 70 percent tax bracket is $300; the "cost" of a similar gift to a person in the 14 percent tax bracket is $860. (If neither chooses to make a deductible gift, the situation would be reversed: after taxes the person in the higher bracket would have only $300 left; the person in the lower bracket would have $860 left.) The allegation of inequity arises because the charitable contribution appears to be worth more to the wealthy person than to the relatively poorer person. But to rest one's entire case against the charitable deduction on this point is to be guilty of over-simplification. There are, in fact, several measures by which a tax system must be evaluated.

We turn again to Bittker's criteria for analyzing the viability of a tax system.[6] He first deals with the allegation of impropriety, which is based upon the consumption theory of tax liability, which in turn holds that one's tax liability should be based upon the amount available for consumption expenditures, taking no account of how one chooses to spend his money. Charitable contributions are, of course, included as a consumption expenditure. Bittker whimsically observes that in such a system tax logic accords a charitable contribution the same classification as wine, women, and song. However, those who advocate this point of view suggest that desirable social objectives may be furthered by a system of matching grants by government. Thus, some expenditures are encouraged, others are not. Bittker notes that there is an inequity in the fact that matching grants may be extended to charitable contributions but not to wine, women, or song, and then asks why, if it is tolerable to achieve social objectives through a matching grant system, it is not equally acceptable to do so through a system of contribution deductions.

He next deals with the criticism that the charitable deduction is inefficient. This view holds that gifts would, for the most part, be made whether or not a deduction is allowed. Because of the importance of recent research we will deal with that subject later in this chapter.

Bittker's final argument attacks the assertion that the tax code fosters inequity. He is not particularly disturbed by the fact that the operation of the charitable contribution tends to reduce progressivity under the tax code. Reference was made above to one study of the 1976 budget which disclosed fifty-one different exemptions or exclusions. It is doubtless this fact which leads Bittker to observe that, while Congress has enacted a progressive tax structure with deductions, it is equally logical to argue that the durable and central features of the tax code are its deductions, and that progression is secondary and expendable. Such a view would not be inconsistent with the basic objectives of any tax structure, which are to raise money necessary for purposes of government and to achieve social and economic goals. He thus concludes that the deduction for charitable contributions is not inconsistent with a progressive rate structure. He goes on to note that the revenue "lost" by virtue of the allowance, can be recovered by increasing rates to which those with higher incomes are subject. He also makes the interesting observation that the charitable deduction actually may increase progressivity by virtue of the fact that it stimulates the transfer of funds from higher- to lower-income taxpayers. The extent of such a redistributive effect is unknown, but substantial gifts to an art museum which may be enjoyed by all without cost, or contributions to a family service agency which then pays the rent obligation of a needy family, are obvious examples.

Another tax expert, Stanley S. Weithorn, approaches this matter of equity from another point of view. In a recent article he notes:

> Many reformers adopt the rather simplistic posture that the primary purpose of tax reform with respect to individual taxpayers is to bring about tax equity by effecting tax equality. I take exception to this premise, since, in reality, there is no such thing as tax equality. It is not possible to create tax equality between, for example, a taxpayer with a $10,000 annual gross income and one with a $200,000 annual gross income; but it is possible to afford each of them (on a comparative basis) tax equity.[7]

On this basis Weithorn believes that reformers should concentrate on elimination from the code of those provisions which support the "tax shelter" industry, leaving the remaining income, estate and gift tax adjustments to be eliminated, revised or retained in light of the social or economic function which those adjustments might serve. In terms of revenue raising, he believes that the focus of tax reform should be directed toward business taxation, particularly the elimination of special benefits afforded to particular industries and to multinational operations.

A draft statement of the Coalition for the Public Good, issued in January 1975, also deals with this matter of equity:

> However, as we have seen, if there were not greater encouragements in the tax system for persons in the higher income brackets to make charitable contributions, they would give appreciably less than they do. As a result, they would retain

more disposable income than they do, and in that key respect, their disparity with people in lower income brackets would actually increase the inequality as the gap between the two groups widens significantly.[8]

In sum, we believe that the matter of progressivity and equity in the tax system, as it affects charitable contributions, must be seen in the context of conflicting values. On the one hand, we favor a tax system which consists of a clear and fair set of guiding principles, of comprehensive and comprehensible laws and regulations that are administered with scrupulous honesty. On the other hand, we must take into account another set of values which grows out of our Judeo-Christian heritage, and which is deeply imbedded in the American pluralistic system. These values are reflected in the number and variety of services to people that are made possible by the voluntary contributions of many individuals.

It finally becomes necessary, therefore, to ask if the contributions deduction is effective. Does it provide an incentive for individual giving, or would most people give the same amount anyway? For years, experienced fund raisers believed and opined that tax incentives did make a difference, especially to large givers.

T. Willard Hunter, in his book, *The Tax Climate for Philanthropy,*[9] reports the reactions of a number of large donors as to how their gifts would be affected if contributions deductions were removed from the tax law. The donors of fifty-three separate gifts totalling $80 million reported that those gifts would have been reduced by 42.5 percent.

The Peterson Commission in its study of foundations, *Foundations, Private Giving, and Public Policy,*[10]

asked eighty-five large donors, "If there were no tax benefits, what effect would it have on your charitable giving?" Ninety-six percent said they would reduce their giving, with a median reduction of 75 percent. Only 4 percent
said that such a change would have no effect on their
giving.

So the matter stood until, in 1972, the 501 (c) (3)
Group resolved to sponsor a serious econometric study of
the actual effects upon giving of the tax deductibility of
contributions. With funds voluntarily subscribed by various philanthropic organizations, the 501 (c) (3) Group
engaged Dr. Martin Feldstein, a professor of Economics
at Harvard University, to conduct the research. It is fair
to note here that the 501 (c) (3) Group took this step with
a certain amount of fear and trepidation, because the possibility existed that objective findings would prove that no
correlation exists between the provision of the tax code
and charitable giving. This would have had the devastat-
ing effect of upsetting assumptions long held and deeply
felt by all of the members of the Group. Fortunately, the
matter had a happy ending! Without going into all the
methodology, findings, limitations and caveats which are
implicit in this kind of research, we find that Feldstein
concludes:

> Eliminating the current deduction of charitable
> contributions would reduce total itemized giving
> by approximately 28 to 56 percent, depending
> upon the particular equation specification. The
> loss on contributions would be relatively greatest
> for educational, medical, and cultural organiza-
> tions. Philanthropies would lose more in the con-
> tributions they receive than the government
> would gain in additional tax revenues. New dis-
> posable income after tax and charitable contribu-

tions would rise in all income groups with the highest percentage increase in the highest income groups.[11]

Professor Feldstein now has extended the basic research which he did for the 501 (c) (3) Group by a further study conducted for the National Commission on Private Philanthropy (the "Filer Commission") and his findings are even more cogent. With the elimination of the charitable deduction, total charitable support from individuals would fall by almost $4.5 billion. Education and hospitals would lose almost 50 percent of their support; social service and cultural programs would see 27 percent and 33 percent, respectively, of their dollars disappear; religion would lose 22 percent of its present contribution receipts. The average gift from individuals would shrink substantially at all income levels. Individuals with $10–$15,000 adjusted gross incomes would cut their average gifts to charity by 22 percent; those with $20–30,000 adjusted gross income, by 40 percent; and those with $50–100,000, by 63 percent.

These findings illuminate one fact that is not widely understood, the unique quality of the charitable contribution, as compared to all other deductible items. The National Assembly for Social Policy and Development first spelled this out in 1963:

> Charitable contributions are discretionary expenditures. One is required to pay state income and sales taxes and local real estate taxes if they apply; in fact all the items that may be deductible are mandatory and required except charitable contributions. One need not make a charitable contribution.
> Charitable contributions are constructive

acts of citizenship. Through them the contributor joins with others in supporting activities which enrich society. Other tax deductible expenditures may or may not have this attribute depending upon circumstances.

Charitable contributions are essentially unselfish acts. The contributor does something for someone else more than for himself. If he borrows working capital for his business or pays interest for the mortgage on his home, he takes steps which give rise to tax deductions. But these steps are for his own or his family's betterment. They might not be selfish expenditures, but they are personal interest expenses.[12]

What the preceding quotation implies is that since the charitable contribution is uniquely different from other deductible expenditures it should be treated differently in the formulation of tax policy. It would be desirable if the charitable contribution could be separated from other deductions so that it would not be associated in the public's mind with tax "loopholes" of any kind.

A proposal to accomplish this has been in the public domain for some time. Why it has not found favor and support within the voluntary sector or within government baffles some observers. In brief, the proposal is that charitable contributions be taken as a deduction from gross income similar to sick pay or the expenses of moving to a new job location, rather than from adjusted gross income. The concept is simple and would go a long way toward removing the charitable contribution from the perennial struggles over tax reform.

The idea first was conceived by Stanley S. Weithorn in the mid-1960s. Although it was discussed with staff members of the Joint Committee on Internal Revenue Taxation of Congress and with leaders of the voluntary sector, the idea lay fallow for a number of years. It was included as a recommendation in the National Assembly's statement of 1972, *Voluntary Giving and Tax Policy—Charity Is Not a Loophole.*[13] It was resurrected by the 501 (c) (3) Group in 1973 when it came under study by a small subcommittee of that group.

The recommendations of the subcommittee, as finally approved by the 501 (c) (3) Group on January 16, 1974, follow:

The Subcommittee recommends:

1. That all charitable contributions, subject to present limitations, be taken as deductions from gross income.
2. That for persons not itemizing, two options be available:

    A. The taxpayer may deduct 20 percent of his allowable Standard Deduction from gross income, (which would reduce his allowable standard deduction by 20 percent)

    or

    B. The taxpayer may itemize and deduct from gross income his actual charitable contributions.

    C. In exercising this option, the taxpayer may take the larger of the two figures.

The Subcommittee believes:

1. That this proposal represents a new and promising approach to the objective sought.
2. That this is an equitable proposal since it makes a deduction from gross income and the

opportunity to itemize available to everyone.
3. Reducing the Standard Deduction by 20 percent, the assumed average of charitable contributions contained therein, will not have any
revenue consequences.[14]

This recommendation reflects the very substantial
difference which exists between deductions for charitable
contributions and all other deductions. Such a move
would isolate and preserve the contribution to a publicly
supported charitable organization from any future statutory changes aimed at modifying the basic concept of
itemized deductions. It would erase the incompatibility
between tax reform and the preservation of the charitable
contribution deduction. And it would free public officials,
both in the Administration and in the Congress, to concentrate on other issues in the field of tax reform without
endangering the future of those organizations which depend on voluntary giving.[15]

In thinking about why this concept has not been
more vigorously promoted one is reminded of the frequently heard lament that "no one speaks for voluntarism." This is true, and we suppose the fact that no one
person or organization does so speak, represents paradoxically both one of the timeless strengths, as well as an
incipient weakness of voluntarism. If any one super organization were to "speak for voluntarism" it would have to
be clothed with such authority and measure of control
that we no longer would have "voluntarism," in the sense
of diffusion and dispersion of effort. The 501 (c) (3) Group
—functioning as a conduit through which information
may be exchanged—and organizations such as the Coalition for the Public Good and the National Center for

Voluntary Action—functioning as occasional coordinators of independent effort—serve effectively to bridge the existing gap.

In concluding this chapter we repeat what we stated earlier. Tax reform is an exceedingly complex matter. Concentration upon elimination of the charitable deduction as a means of achieving a measure of equity and simplification must be weighed against the ultimate effect, i.e., the reduction in voluntary giving which inevitably would follow would produce a cataclysmic effect upon the voluntary institutional fabric of our society.

To some extent, this represents a familiar picture of a deep conflict in values. On the one side is the comment of an American representative at the Ditchley Conference on "Philanthropy in the 70's: An Anglo-American Discussion," who said, "I challenge the democracy and the morality of any tax incentive for philanthropy. I challenge the idea of the superiority of private philanthropy over the democratic process."[16] On the other side, and in our view, one of the highest moral values to which we can collectively aspire is the preservation and strengthening of our voluntary institutions, one indispensable means to which is the preservation and enhancement of the tax deductibility of the charitable contribution.

NOTES

1. WILLIAMS, MYERS and QUIGGLE, Attorneys and Counselors at Law, Washington, D.C., Memorandum, February 12, 1975, p. 3. (Typewritten.)
2. The National Assembly for Social Policy and Development, Inc., Official Position Statement, *Voluntary Giving and Tax Policy, Charity Is Not a Loophole* (New York: National Assembly for Social Policy and Development, 1972), p. 9.
3. BORIS I. BITTKER, "The Propriety and Vitality of a Federal Income Tax Deduction for Private Philanthropy" (Paper presented at the Tax Institute Symposium on the Impact of Taxes on Philanthropy, Washington, D.C., December 2–3, 1971), p. 6.
4. Ibid., p. 8.
5. Ibid., p. 11.
6. Ibid., pp. 12–13.
7. STANLEY S. WEITHORN, "Comments on Tax Justice Act of 1975" (New York, January 13, 1975), p. 2. (Typewritten.)
8. Coalition for the Public Good, "The Charitable Deduction: A Statement on the Roles of the Government and the Voluntary Sector," Alexandria, Virginia, January 6, 1975, p. 12. (Mimeographed.)
9. T. WILLARD HUNTER, *The Tax Climate for Philanthropy* (Washington, D.C.: American College Public Relations Association, 1968), p. 118.
10. Commission on Foundations and Private Philanthropy, *Foundations, Private Giving, and Public Policy* (Chicago: University of Chicago Press, 1970), p. 34.
11. MARTIN S. FELDSTEIN, "On the Effects of the Income Tax Treatment of Charitable Contributions: Some Preliminary Results" (Harvard University, Cambridge, Massachusetts, December 1973), p. 37. (Mimeographed.)
12. The National Assembly for Social Policy and Development,

Inc., op. cit., p. 12.

13. Ibid., p. 14.
14. 501 (c) (3) Group, "Report of the Subcommittee" (Washington, D.C., January 16, 1974), p. 1. (Mimeographed.)
15. The National Assembly for Social Policy and Development, Inc., op. cit., p. 15.
16. JOHN J. CORSON and HARRY V. HODSON, eds., *Philanthropy in the 70's: An Anglo-American Discussion,* (New York: The Council on Foundations, Inc., 1973), p. 13.

6 BACK TO ADVOCACY

THE MATTER OF permissible legislative activity must be set in the broader context of the extent of commitment of a voluntary organization to influencing public policy. What is the agency's view of itself and its mission? Should the organization devote its entire resources and energies to giving service, or should it be concerned both with those it serves and with those conditions within the community inimical to those it serves and which detract from the quality of life of the community? In other words, is it prepared to influence public policy? This question identifies a theme that has run intermittently throughout the history of voluntarism, extending back to the Roman and Greek experience and heightened in the late nineteenth and early twentieth centuries by many of the social reform efforts.

Concern with social reform assumes an interrelatedness between the individual and the social systems and the institutions which surround him. It implies that the welfare of the individual cannot be isolated from that of the community, so that to serve one without concern for the other may be of little or no avail. It portends a responsibility on the part of the agency, arising from its experience in serving people, to move from case to cause, and to register concern for those external forces and conditions which bring people to the agency, and which adversely affect their ability to function. This view conceives of the agency, not as an "agency in the community" but as a "community agency."

Such a formulation frees us from the grip of definitional precision. Whether one talks about advocacy, influencing public social policy, engaging in social action, or promoting institutional change makes no essential difference. The objectives sought may be many and diverse (from the activities of a neighborhood group to get a stop light at a dangerous school intersection to promotion of national health insurance) and the repertoire of activities directed to achieving the goal may be similarly varied (from peaceful group protests to expert testimony before a Congressional committee). One of the unique characteristics of voluntarism is its ability to mobilize individual and group effort toward those objectives which are felt to be important to the participants.

Pifer, in the 1974 Annual Report of the Carnegie Corporation, refers to the complexity of public policy:

> The processes which lead up to the formal enactment of public policy in this country are extraordinarily complex. It is a deliberate part of our system that these processes are thrown open to wide citizen participation, involving inputs from, and interaction among, elected and appointed officials, political parties, the communications media, industry, trade associations, trade unions, professional associations, citizen action and many other groups, and, finally, the charitable sector with its wide range of private, non-profit organizations.[1]

In travelling around the country, one of the most visible and audible signs is the impulsion of many persons toward activism and institutional change. People want to be where the action is, they want to influence and help shape the forces of change. And it is volunteers themselves who are expressing the belief that voluntary agencies not only have an obligation to give service of the highest quality, but also have a responsibility to witness, to be advocates, and to speak out affirmatively, even militantly, on issues that affect their constituencies.

The assumptions and stirrings observed expose some complex issues. A simple statement of an organization's responsibility to those it serves is insufficient. One must probe more deeply. Are there philosophical reasons, intrinsic to the legal status, values, and authentic role of voluntary agencies which should cause them to be concerned with institutional and social change? We believe there are, and would like to focus on several aspects of these reasons.

One eloquently expressed view on the subject is that of Paul Sherry, in an editorial in the *Journal of Current Social Issues* of July-August 1970:

> The primary role of voluntary associations in American life is to continually shape and reshape the vision of a more just social order, to propose programs which might lead to the manifestation of that vision, to argue for them with other contenders in the public arena, and to press for adoption and implementation. For a voluntary association to do less than this is to abdicate its responsibility.[2]

A year later he has this to say about that statement:

> The basic assumption of this definition is that voluntary associations are necessary to help our nation remain viable, honest, and responsive to

human need. Without effective voluntary associations these qualities will disappear from our public life—obsolescence will replace viability,
deception will replace honesty, and indifference
will replace responsiveness. Although strong
voluntary associations will not, by themselves,
assure a healthy nation, sickness is certain to pre-
vail without them. The reinvigoration of the
voluntary sector will, therefore, go a long way
toward the rebirth of the nation's total life.[3]

Sherry is saying that when faith, morale, and confidence
in all our institutions are at a perilously low point, as
indeed they are today, one can still look to the voluntary
sector as an invigorating force for all of society because it
remains the repository of values which Americans have
traditionally held dear. The problem is to make sure that
those values are applied to the problems, issues, and
choices which society faces.

Ronald Borod, in his pamphlet, *Lobbying for the
Public Interest,* approaches the problem from a legal point
of view:

The overriding principle embodied in the first
amendment is the right of dissent. "The First
Amendment means . . . that the only constitutional way our government can preserve itself is
to leave its people the fullest possible freedom to
praise, criticize or discuss, as they see fit, all governmental policies. . . ." (*Barenblatt v. United
States,* 360 U.S. 109, 145) Another principle,
closely related to and in certain ways deriving
from the first amendment, and which has provided an important strand in the fabric of our

national life, is pluralism. In a country such as ours, where more and more functions are being performed by a strong central government, it is becoming increasingly important that incentives be given to members of the private sector to develop alternative or competing solutions to social problems, or at least to have their own ideas incorporated into solutions undertaken by the Government.[4]

An interesting analysis of the legal status of voluntary organizations comes from Professor James Luther Adams of the Andover Newton Theological School, a theologian and one of the outstanding students of voluntary associations. In May 1971, having referred to the separation of powers articulated in the Constitution and having referred to the first and the ninth amendments, the latter of which reserves to the people those rights not specifically enumerated in the Constitution, Adams observes:

Here we see, then, a kind of separation of powers between the government and the people, a recognition that the community possesses a broader jurisdiction than the state. (The State is the creature and not the creator of the community.) This constitutionally-sanctioned separation gives autonomy to voluntary associations as well as to volunteers in these associations. Indeed, voluntary associations as an arm of the community have not only the intrinsic right to exist; they may also criticize the government and attempt to affect its policies. The denial of this right is the first mark of totalitarianism.[5]

Why should one accept, as we do, the moral and legal obligation and responsibility of voluntary organizations to be concerned with influencing social policy? In the final analysis it will be because there will be work to do in the next decade or so. We see at least three major societal changes taking place in the shaping of which the input and influence of the voluntary sector could be critical in the immediate future and beyond.

The first change arises from the fact that, more and more, major decisions affecting all people will be political decisions. An increasingly powerful political system will articulate goals, formulate options, determine priorities, and allocate resources. Daniel Bell predicts that there will be a greater passing of power to the President, and that the presidency will become, as he describes it, a system of free action, choosing which interests it allows to be heard, and engaging in free bargaining with various interest groups. This accretion of governmental power will be tempered and influenced by the right of people to affect those decisions which control their lives.[6] (It is debatable whether, as an aftermath of Watergate, the trend toward increased presidential power has been arrested.)

The second concerns the extent to which the United States will be increasingly drawn into collaboration and common cause with other nations of the world to relieve hunger, reduce poverty, share medical knowledge and skills, and collaborate in establishing educational programs. It cannot be long before everyone realizes, as someone put it, that we live in a very small world, and that our economic, social, ecological, and political stability is inextricably bound up with what happens everywhere in the world. Nor can the United States, as it has in the past, adopt either an isolationist or a paternalistic posture in its relationship with the peoples of other countries. Just as the day of the Lady Bountiful is past in American charity, so is the day of the Lord Bountiful past in international charity. As it is widely accepted now in our country that individuals have a right to participation in those decisions affecting them, so it is that other countries have a right to participate in decisions affecting them, as well as in how those decisions are implemented. One of the authors was shocked recently while talking to an engineer who was en route to India to help establish an irrigation system. He doubted the success of his mission "because those people are so ignorant you can't tell them a damned thing."

The third force which looms in the future is the insistent yearning of more and more people for an improvement in the quality of their own life and living. The quality of life runs a gamut of concepts; the search for individual meaning and identity; the desire for an unpolluted environment; the impulse to dedicate more of one's self in service to others: the wish to be creative through artistic self-expression; and the longing for more free time in order to exercise individual and personal choices with respect to what one does. One's mind goes back to the early sixties when the specter of automation led people and organizations into a frantic search for a list of constructive things to do with the soon-to-be achieved leisure time. Now, it would appear, the impulse to improve the quality of life is much more fundamental. It goes to the question of national goals and priorities, and it extends all the way from, for example, improved library services to a national social report which would measure the extent to which goals in health, education, income maintenance, and the absence of crime have been achieved.

Taken in the aggregate these three subjects—the increasing centrality of political decision-making, the responsibility of the United States within a global setting, and the increasing desire for improvement in the quality of life—represent a formidable agenda of concerns for all Americans. Yet the forecast with respect to the political system holds out hope. Indeed, one reason for the alienation and apathy of many citizens is their seeming lack of ability to influence political processes and decisions. Certainly an annual, biennial, or quadrennial election represents an important civic responsibility, but hardly an effective method of influencing the rapidly moving course of events in Washington, Sacramento, or San Antonio. Letters to public officials are likewise important, but their influence is probably marginal, and too often those who write receive a courteous form of response and may then be placed on the official's mailing list for reports of future achievements. The medium of the future through which influence will most directly be felt is through the group, organization, or association—sometimes singly, perhaps more often in coalition with like-minded organizations. The individual impact is thereby multiplied by a factor of z in the official's mind to represent a force to be taken into account in his or her constitutency.

Thus the organizations of which we speak in this book—the thousands of philanthropic organizations which have their legal base in the first amendment—have a means of influence, a constituency, experience in the day-to-day conduct of their affairs, and a set of values which can and, we believe, must be applied to the issues which will face our country in the immediate future. Not to do so, will be an abdication to other forces, perhaps motivated by an entirely different set of values. To do so is to contribute to what we all hope will be a more just, equitable, and peaceful society.

As we have implied, there are organizations which do not believe that their mission encompasses the influencing of public policy. Other organizations may feel differently about their mission, but be reluctant to engage in actual or possible controversy. We appreciate this concern. Obviously, a decision to embark on a course of action that invites serious controversy must be carefully evaluated by each agency in each situation. We appreciate, too, the perils of controversy and feel strongly that controversy merely for its own sake is counterproductive. Nevertheless, we do suggest that when an organization has adopted a course of action based upon a firm set of values it may find that controversy has united the organization, enhanced its public image, improved its staff morale, and even increased its fund-raising potential.

Organizations wishing to influence public policy can choose from many methods. Among them is legislative action. Because the Internal Revenue Code places limits upon the ability of an agency to influence legislation, many agencies feel that their role as an advocate for change is limited and they abandon the field. Nothing could be further from the truth, as we shall see. It is necessary to deal with the matter of permissible legislative action, because the provisions of the Code act as a deterrent to those organizations which may wish to say something about a piece of legislation which is germane to the purposes for which they are organized.

The applicable section of the Code, Section 501 (c) (3), in referring to organizations which receive most of their money directly or indirectly as contributions from the general public, grants tax exemption only to an organization "no substantial part of the activities of which is carrying on propaganda, or otherwise attempting, to influence legislation."[10] Similarly applicable is Section 170 of the Code, which allows a deduction, subject to certain limitations, for charitable contributions, and Section 170

(c) (2) (D), which defines charitable contributions so as to include contributions to organizations "no substantial part of the activities of which is carrying on propaganda, or otherwise attempting, to influence legislation."

The Regulations, in defining what is meant by influencing legislation, say that an organization will be regarded as attempting to influence legislation if it a) contacts or urges the public to contact members of a legislative body to propose, support, or oppose legislation, or b) advocates the adoption or rejection of legislation, which is defined to include federal, state, or local. The Regulations also define an "action" organization, which is not tax exempt. Its characteristics are: 1) Its main or primary objectives (as distinguished from incidental or secondary) may be attained only by the enactment or defeat of legislation. 2) It advocates or campaigns for the attainment of such objectives (as distinguished from nonpartisan analysis, research, or study, and making the results available to the public).

The real problem in living with the Code is what is meant by the phrase "no substantial part of the activities of which." Neither the Regulations nor any judicial decisions have suggested a formula for determining whether an amount of activity is substantial or insubstantial, or for that matter, what is meant by "activities." For example, does this include time, or costs? Does it require an imputed time for volunteers or board members? It is doubtful if any such formula could or ever will be formulated because this is a factual question dependent upon all of the circumstances in a particular case. It is worth noting that the dedication of something less than five percent of the time and effort of an organization to legislative activity "could not be deemed substantial within the meaning of the section" (*Seasongood v. Commissioner,* 227 F. 2nd 907 6th Circ. 1955).

The situation is unclear and ambiguous, and thus acts as a deterrent to action. Organizations which consult legal counsel more often than not will get a very cautious opinion as to their rights under the Code. Moreover, the ambiguity of the Code invites selective enforcement by the Internal Revenue Service. An organization may be reviewed because its activities came to the personal attention of someone in the Service, an agency may come up for review because of publicity, sought or unsought, or the Service may act because of a complaint from a Congressman or other public official who feels aggrieved by the activities of an organization.

The following excerpt from the testimony of the president of the National Assembly for Social Policy and Development before the House Ways and Means Committee in May 1972 is in point:

> Permit me to refer to three specific situations which emphasize this problem. Recently, for example, the head of the Exempt Organization Section of a major district office of the Internal Revenue Service said to a group of approximately 25 executives of national voluntary social welfare organizations that serious consideration was being given to what he termed the "Impact Test" by which exempt status would be determined by the outcome of legislative activities. In other words, an agency would presumably be subject to penalty for success.
>
> The confused state of administration of a statute which engenders great uncertainty is illustrated by the recent example of the Young

Women's Christian Association of New Castle County, Delaware. On January 17, 1972 the District Director proposed a revocation of exempt status of the organization on grounds of legislative activity. On February 22, 1972 on the basis of "further consideration" of Forms 990-A for 1968 and 1969 the Internal Revenue Service advised that "the proposal made in the letter of January 17 is hereby withdrawn." The letter noted that the activities of the agency included the formation of a Public Affairs Committee, contacting members of the legislature "on a number of occasions," and that these activities increased in frequency in 1969. The agency was cautioned about loss of exempt status in the future if attempts to influence legislation became a substantial part of its operation.

In still another instance an organization which wishes not to be identified was advised by the District Director of the Internal Revenue Service following an examination of records for 1968, 1969, and 1970 that no change in exempt status was being proposed, but that the following activities (among others) were "objectionable to the status" of a section 501 (c) (3) organization, presumably because there was a legislative purpose: "Your vehicle was used to transport several of your employees to a convention in Denver, Colorado. There is no evidence in your records to show that the purpose of the trip constituted an exempt activity. . . . During the years under examination you adopted a general program of 'community involvement' without notifying the District Director of your change in operations . . . Records were not maintained to show that activities of your executive director and commu-

nity organizations were in furtherance of your
exempt purpose."[7]

These three illustrations are supplied, not to offer
criticism of the Internal Revenue Service, but to support
the contention that the effect of the ambiguous character
of existing law is felt by everyone: by the Internal Revenue
Service which is irresistibly drawn toward selective enforcement; and by voluntary organizations which see the
law and the Internal Revenue Service's inconsistent enforcement efforts as imposing unreasonable and uninten-
tionally narrow limits on legislative activity.

Several attempts have been made to correct this
situation by amendments to the Internal Revenue Code.
Beginning in 1971 with identical bills introduced by Senator Muskie and Congressman Symington, succeeding bills
have been introduced in the Senate by Senators Muskie
and Scott, and in the House by Congressmen Ullman and
Conable. The original Muskie bill would have allowed a
501 (c) (3) organization to deal directly with legislatures
on matters of direct interest to the organization, and to
communicate with its members or contributors with respect to legislative matters of direct interest to the organization or its contributors. The legislative activities permitted are comparable to those for which a taxpayer is
entitled to a deduction in connection with his trade or
business. So-called grass roots lobbying (attempts to influence the general public) would have been prohibited.

Beginning with the Ullman bill introduced in 1972
an effort was made to achieve precision in defining and
allowing legislative activity. Under the bill 20 percent of
an organization's expenditures would be allowable, provided it was related to the organization's purposes, and 5

percent of the 20 percent could be devoted to grass roots activity.

The arguments which emerged from the Administration in opposition seemed to be derived from singularly ill-founded conclusions. One was that since the voluntary sector now spends, in the aggregate, about thirty billion dollars a year, passage of the Ullman bill would immediately release six billion dollars (20 percent) for lobbying, and Congress would be submerged with lobbyists. This argument ignored the fact that voluntary agencies were not likely to divert 20 percent of their funds to legislative activity under any foreseeable circumstances, that their primary mission was service, and that legislative activity was, in their minds, clearly ancillary. The 20 percent figure had been picked to provide an outside figure within which an organization would operate without fear of losing exempt status if a particularly crucial issue were to arise. Indeed, there are some who worry about whether, if present restraints were modified, lobbying might not become the sole purpose of an organization at the expense of regular service. If this proved to be so, the organization would be compelled to surrender its present legal classification under the Code and would become an "action" organization, to which contributions would not be deductible in tax reporting.

During testimony an Administration spokesman also advanced the view that the real problem was one of "balancing" public and business interests, and that voluntary agencies should be allowed to communicate with a legislator only when there was a competing interest between the two. The rationale of this point eluded most observers. This response further emphasizes the present inequity between the restrictions imposed on voluntary nonprofit organizations and the liberal provisions of Section 162 (e) which extended in 1962 to businesses and the organizations which represent them the freedom to conduct legislative efforts with tax deductible funds. At that time the Senate Finance Committee explained the grounds for its action in these words:

> It is also desirable that taxpayers who have information bearing on the impact of present laws, or proposed legislation on their trade or business not be discouraged in making the information available to the members of the Congress or legislators in other levels of government. The presentation of such information to the legislators is necessary to a proper evaluation on their part of the impact of present or proposed legislation.[8]

We believe that the information and views of voluntary organizations on matters of public policy should also be available to legislative bodies. Many voluntary organizations have knowledge, expertise, and experience arising from decades of dedicated concern for people and the social ills which beset our society. There are, of course, those who argue that the nonprofit field should not be compared to business in this respect because business generates tax revenues and the nonprofit field does not. This is only one side of the coin; the other side is that the nonprofit field saves the government money by doing what otherwise, in many cases, would be demanded of government! The glaring inequity in the present situation is best illustrated by the fact that the members of the business community can deduct their lobbying expenses, while all others cannot, even with respect to the same legislation. Subsequent legislation introduced by Congressman Conable and by others has attempted to deal with some of the inequities and ambiguities in these problem areas. One provision would allow a decreasing percentage of allowable legislative activity as an organization's budget increases. This may reduce the prospect of a swarm of lobbyists descending on Washington, but it does appear to some to be needlessly complex. Another provision allows for an organization to elect whether it wishes to be covered, or to continue under the present provisions of the Code. Some organizations are so large, or so powerful, that they can function adequately under the present law, without an election process that might cause them to be subject to subsequent review.

The matter of grass roots lobbying has always been complex, because of, on the one hand, the reluctance of Congress to permit organizations to appeal to the general public, and, on the other hand, the difficulty in defining the constituency or membership to which an organization might legitimately appeal. Is it anyone who contributes to the support of the organization? Who subscribes to a publication? Or who buys cookies? This matter may now be resolved by use of the phrase, "bona fide members," which presumably refers to individuals who have achieved some legal relationship to the organization as provided in the organization's by-laws or other official definition of membership.

The final matter of concern is the status of churches and integrated auxiliaries. Because U.S. churches do not acknowledge the right of any civil authority to restrict or control their ability to witness on any subject, they quite properly do not wish to come under the provisions of any law, by either choice or compulsion. Church organizations do not object to other voluntary organizations having the benefit of amendments to the law; nor do they wish to oppose a proposed new law on the grounds of its special impact upon them. Hence, for them, exclusion from provisions of the proposed bill would seem to be preferable to a posture of benevolent neutrality, which might be difficult to maintain.

Strangely enough, the section of the Internal Revenue Code bearing upon legislative activity of voluntary organizations was passed in 1934 without debate, and represented the retaliation of one United States Senator against a single organization. Even the sparse records that exist suggest that difficulties of drafting caused the provision to be broader than was intended. Senator Reed had this to say in 1934:

> There is no reason in the world why a contribution made to the National Economy League should be deductible as if it were a charitable contribution if it is a selfish one made to advance the personal interests of the giver of the money. That is what the committee was trying to reach; but we found great difficulty in phrasing the amendment. I do not reproach the draftsmen. I think we gave them an impossible task; but this amendment goes much further than the committee intended to go.[9]

Ronald Borod, in his article cited above, also speaks to the legislative history of the substantiality provision:

> What the legislative history suggests, then, is that some members of Congress, even in 1934, were aware of the distinction between public interest and private interest groups, and were concerned that the latter might obtain tax benefits intended

only for the former. That is, the substantiality test
was not an expression of any congressional determination that political activities are inherently
inconsistent with charitable status, but rather a
decision by Congress that the tax benefits intended for charitable and educational organizations should not be converted to the use of private
interest groups.[10]

It is also worth noting that government programs were
small in 1934 and Congress had no reason to foresee the
future important role of voluntary organizations and citizens in attempting to influence a greatly expanding and
increasingly complex and remote governmental system.

The final and convincing argument against the present provisions on substantiality is also cited by Borod. He
notes how important it is that incentives be given to members of the private sector to develop alternative or competing solutions to social problems, especially when more and
more functions are being performed by a strong central
government. He asserts that it is exactly such incentives
that sections 501 and 170 of the Code were intended to
provide:

While it is recognized that tax exemption involves
a form of public subsidy, it is one which permits
individual citizens, corporations, and organized
philanthropic groups to determine the kind and
variety of programs they wish to support and
develop on their own initiative. This permits
quick response to developing needs, experimentation in methods of meeting those needs, and a
wide variety of independent services with a maximum of citizen participation.[11]

Yet the irony of the situation is that the proscriptions of the sections of the Code which prohibit substantial legislative activity have the anomalous result of discouraging conduct which the sections as a whole were intended to sanction.

One problem with the Code is that its impact with respect to substantiality is so depressing that individuals and organizations may forget that there are other sections of the Code that may be utilized to foster communication between an organization and a legislative body. The following activities are not defined or construed by the Code as representing legislative activity:

1. Testimony provided by request of the legislative body, which aims to take advantage of the organization's expertise and knowledge in a given field. One observer commented that this was a loophole big enough to drive a truck through. In fact, however, it is not. While appearances before a legislative body can be "arranged" it is much more likely to be the controversial character of the testimony that will or will not get an organization into trouble. And it is difficult to avoid controversial issues in today's society.

2. The preparation of technical analyses which emphasize probable outcome of proposed legislation, or stress the impact of present laws.

3. Presentations (defined as educational within the Regulations) which may advocate a particular position or viewpoint, but present a sufficiently fair and full exposition of pertinent facts to permit an individual or the public to form an independent opinion or conclusion. The problem with this is that it is a useful technique within limits, implying as it does the absence of a position or of recommendations which are vigorously advanced.

And then finally, two additional types of activities

fall outside the meaning of legislative activity, as defined within the Code:

1. Legislative activity by an organization bearing on its own tax exempt status. Included within the scope of this exception are issues of tax reform bearing on the deductibility of charitable contributions and measures relating to a change in the limits of permissible legislative activity.

2. Efforts to influence the rules and regulations by which legislation is to be administered. This is most important because legislation is usually passed in broad, enabling terms, and the rules and regulations, which have the full force of law when they are promulgated, become very important.

There are some additional considerations which organizations will wish to take into account, assuming that they set out to influence public policy within the context of the present, or any future law. The first is that the function itself must be internally differentiated, within the organization. Except for very small agencies, the function of public policy should be structurally defined within the agency and should be the particular responsibility, even on a part-time basis, of designated staff. It is not something which can be done effectively as an ancillary part of another function. And, as we have seen, there are many ways in which policy can be affected beyond engaging in legislative activity. The important thing is that the function be accorded an organizational rank which will make it parallel with the service function.

Another element, perhaps more important than much of what we have said, is that an organization utilize what Max L. Stackhouse calls the "reserve of influence" concept.[12] This recognizes the importance of the agency's own constituency, whether it be of individuals or of organizations, becoming familiar with the important issues, of developing sensitivity to and a felt competence in the grasp and understanding of issues. A constituency thus becomes what Stackhouse calls a "low visibility power"— available to be mobilized in behalf of an agency's position, but also able as individuals to exercise influence in other organizations to which they invariably belong, or of simply acting on their own initiative. For an agency to implement this approach successfully calls for a systematic and careful program of analysis of issues and legislation, tracing the status of legislation, responsible factual and technical analysis of problems and their impact on persons served by the agency, and so forth. It should be conceived as an ongoing part of the agency program, involving continuous education in contrast to a sporadic and emergency appeal to one's constituency to "get to your Congressman and urge him or her to support (or oppose) this bill."[13]

An issue which will probably never be resolved is that of expertise as opposed to power. Is it more desirable for someone making a presentation to a Congressional committee, for example, to speak from a posture of being a recognized expert on a particular subject, or is it preferable to represent a constituency which is sufficiently impressive in size to attract a legislator's attention? Generally, the weight seems to fall on the side of representing power through a constituency, because it is difficult to find spokesmen who possess the requisite expertise to give testimony, and to respond to questions in the depth and scope frequently asked in the dialogue which usually follows direct testimony. Naturally, we would hope that one might have the best of both worlds—that an organization represent an informed and impressive constituency, and that the presentor be of sufficient stature and knowledge to be able effectively to field any questions. But for the moment, the power of the constituency doubtless preempts the field.

An example of the power of a constituency is seen in the following anecdote.

> A twenty-year effort to establish a school of social work appeared to hinge on a meeting arranged with the Governor and an interested group of citizens. The Governor's views were unknown in advance. As the delegation was being introduced to the Governor, he drew one person aside and said how much he had appreciated that individual's support in the recent election. Was there anything he could do for him? Said the friend, "Yes, we want a school of social work." Replied the Governor, "Alright, you have it!" And he was as good as his word.

An example in which both expertise and the power of a constituency were lacking is to be found in this anecdote.

> A presentation supporting a departmental budget was to be made to a state legislative committee. A prominent layman agreed to make the presentation, and did a masterful job. When he was finished, members of the committee asked penetrating questions which he found he couldn't answer. He found himself in a most embarrassing position, and soon resigned from the board of the organization. He should certainly not have been placed in the position of being a "front" for the organization. He should have been fully briefed by staff and ready for most questions with available technical back-up.

In the pursuit of public policy goals, it is not uncommon for an organization to adopt a broad statement of policy on a particular issue which then may serve as a framework or rubric within which the organization can take a stand on particular issues as they arise. Generally, an organization's actions or representations must be timely if they are to be effective, and it is not always possible to convene the board or the responsible committee to take appropriate action. Hence the desirability of broad policy statements within which specific action can be taken.

In the process of acting to approve broad policy statements the organization must take care not to sink to the lowest possible denominator of consensus in order to reach agreement. As boards become less homogeneous and more representative of diverse community interests this problem may come increasingly to the fore. And in consequence a statement may become so watered down as to be virtually meaningless. At least two organizations, the Committee on Economic Development and the National Assembly for Social Policy and Development, found a solution to the problem. That was to make provision for written exceptions to a proposed policy. Thus, any individual who disagrees with a section of the proposed policy (and usually such disagreements seem to be directed to just a part of a statement) could enter a caveat or disagreement which is then attached to, and made part of, the official policy, either as a footnote, or at the end. In this manner, a stronger policy can be approved, individuals can speak their minds, and the organization has a much firmer foundation on which to act.

We hope we have made our biases clear in this chapter. We believe that there is a legal and moral obligation incumbent upon every voluntary agency to utilize its experience and to apply its values to the issues and problems of the day via a differentially structured and internally supported program of influencing social policy, thereby using the weight and stature of the organization as a lever for social change. To do less is to disregard one of the prime opportunities and justifications for the existence of the voluntary organization.

NOTES

1. ALAN PIFER, "Report of the President," in the *Annual Report of the Carnegie Corporation,* (New York: Carnegie Corporation, 1974), p. 3.
2. PAUL H. SHERRY, "Getting It Together," *Journal of Current Social Issues,* 9 (Autumn 1971), p. 2.
3. Ibid.
4. RONALD S. BOROD, "Lobbying for the Public Interest—Federal Tax Policy and Administration," 42 *New York University Law Review,* p. 1103.
5. JAMES LUTHER ADAMS, "Voluntary Associations in Search of Identity," *Journal of Current Social Issues,* 9 (Autumn 1971), p. 17.
6. DANIEL BELL, *The Coming of Post-Industrial Society* (New York: Basic Books, Inc., 1973).
7. U.S. Congress, House Committee on Ways and Means, *Legislative Activity by Certain Types of Exempt Organizations,* Hearings on H.R. 13720, 92nd Cong., 2nd sess., 1972.
8. Ibid., p. 66
9. SENATOR DAVID A. REED, 78 Cong. Rec. 5861 (1934), cited in Ronald S. Borod, op.cit., p. 1114.
10. RONALD S. BOROD, op.cit., p. 1114.
11. Ibid., p. 1103
12. MAX L. STACKHOUSE, *Journal of Current Social Issues,* 9 Autumn 1971.
13. For a comprehensive approach to "advocacy," cf. ELLEN MANSER, ed. *Family Advocacy: A Manual for Action* (New York: Family Service Association of America, 1973).

7 THE MONEY CRUNCH

THE MONEY PROBLEM is acute for the simple reason that the cost of doing business is outrunning income. Storm warnings have been up for some time, but people on the shore may not have noticed that many boats have trimmed sails and battened down hatches, and that some are in serious distress.

In the 1970 Annual Report of the Carnegie Corporation, Pifer says:

> . . . a high proportion of our private educational, cultural, health, and welfare institutions are heading into deep trouble, increasingly affected by social and economic forces they are powerless to withstand. The steady, unrelenting deterioration of their position has now, for the first time, raised doubts about the continued viability of our traditional system of shared responsibility between public and private endeavor. For varying reasons, the American people at large and most of their political leaders seem either unaware of the situation, or unconcerned. In an age noted for the gravity and complexity of its problems, this problem, as important as many with which we are currently obsessed, has simply failed to make its mark on the national consciousness.[1]

The Annual Report of the American Association of Fund-Raising Counsel, *Giving 1971,* has this to say:

.... organizations and institutions ... are still experiencing increased costs beyond expectations. Labor costs are hurting both education and health dramatically. Both areas live with 10% inflation factors, as do the churches. To counteract this, faculty are not rehired, and cost cutting is common for all non-profit organizations today.[2]

The magazine, *Institutional Investor,* in an editorial in August 1972, declares:

Aside from the occasional news story about a college or a museum that has come upon hard times, the financial crisis now confronting this nation's nonprofit institutions has gone largely untold. Yet it is real, pervasive and significant. The ravages of inflation have been taking their toll of non-profits, the soaring costs of the services they aim to provide far outpacing their income from endowments, private and public giving and other sources. And at stake is nothing less than America's entire system of private institutions.[3]

And finally, George P. Shultz, Secretary of the Treasury, and Wilbur D. Mills, Chairman of the House Ways and Means Committee, said upon the formation of the Commission on Private Philanthropy and Public Needs, on November 5, 1973:

Our society has never been more affluent; but the private educational, cultural, research, and welfare institutions that give it much of its strength

and quality are in dire straits. Many are confronted by large deficits and often by threats to
their very existence.[4]

Consider that these warnings were issued when the
price index was increasing, beginning in 1970, at an annual rate of 5.9, 4.2, and 3.3. By the time that inflation had
reached double digit proportions, the problem had become even more serious. One needed only to read the
newspapers to find daily evidence of the problem: "Decline Is Found in Support for Schools," "Social Action Hit
By Financial Woes," "Conferees Weigh Museum Crisis,"
and "Shrinking Giants," referring to the reduction in market value of foundation assets.

The increased cost of doing business has included
items that are familiar to all of us: the cost of gas and
electricity, of housing, of communication by telephone or
mail, the increased cost of food. But there are additional
factors which have a profound impact on voluntary organizations of all kinds. Perhaps the most important is the
fact that philanthropic services of all kinds are labor intensive, in contrast to manufacturing enterprises, which are
capital intensive. The Peterson report notes that personnel
costs and related expenses of fifty Chicago philanthropic
institutions were, in 1968, 66 percent of total costs, compared to U.S. manufacturing establishments, in which
comparable items were only 24 percent of costs.[5] As the
report points out, philanthropy's "financial condition is
thus particularly vulnerable to increases in the costs of the
labor its employs—again in contrast to manufacturing
enterprises, which can materially offset increases in labor
rates by using new technologies which increase production." And, as specialized knowledge expands, along with

personnel standards and salaries, so will the problems increase in labor intensive fields.

The Peterson report goes on to compare increases in salaries of employees of Chicago charitable organizations with those of U.S. production workers during the period 1963 to 1968. While the salary of the average U.S. production worker in manufacturing increased by only 23 percent during this time, the increases in salaries of employees of charitable institutions were as follows: hospital interns, 81 percent; musicians, 55 percent; nurses, 49 percent; university professors, 37 percent; social workers, 38 percent; executive directors, 32 percent; and librarians, 28 percent. In a situation where salaries are seriously depressed to begin with two forces are at work. The first is increasing recognition that employees of voluntary organizations should not be expected, because of their dedication and commitment to the cause for which they are working, to work for below-normal salaries. The second factor is that their salaries begin to reflect favorable union contracts. Another factor that contributes heavily to the increase in total personnel costs has been the sharp increase in fringe benefits and in their costs, especially medical and retirement benefits.

And finally, it is not possible for philanthropic organizations to pass on increased costs to the consumer in the same way or to the same degree that manufacturing organizations can in a reasonably free, flexible, and open market. Of the fifty voluntary organizations in the one locality surveyed for the Peterson Report, the median income from fees was 14 percent of total income. During the 1963–68 period covered by the survey, organizations had substantially increased their fees, as follows: YWCA of Greater Chicago class fees, 53 percent; Visiting Nurse Association of Chicago visits, 121 percent; University of

Chicago tuition, 44 percent; Art Institute of Chicago tuition, 38 percent; Chicago Symphony Orchestra balcony tickets, 35 percent; Girl Scouts of Greater Chicago camp fees, 18 percent; Michael Reese Hospital day rates, 109 percent; and Chicago Youth Center camp fees, 43 percent. Nevertheless, the report observes, the costs of service increased faster than the increase in income from fees. The report concludes that it is highly unlikely that fees will ever account for more than 14 percent of the total income of the organizations taken as a whole.

One reason for this, of course, is that, at a certain point, increases in fees tend to become counterproductive, excluding from access to service many persons for whom the service is intended, frequently low- and middle-income persons. While this outcome can be obviated to some extent by a sliding fee schedule, the essential problem remains. Hence some mechanism for sharing costs among those members of the community who indirectly benefit from the existence of the service must be found. Theoretically the most equitable method of achieving this objective is through the use of tax dollars, which would, however, destroy voluntarism as we know it today.

Within the health and welfare portion of the voluntary sector, at the present time the most equitable method of achieving a sharing of costs, and of "finding the money where it is and spending it where it is needed," is through federated fund-raising mechanisms, of which the largest is the United Way. But the United Way movement itself is having difficulty in keeping up with the march of inflation. For the first time, in 1974 contributions to all United Ways in the United States and Canada exceeded one billion dollars. But while this is a significant accomplishment, increases in giving from year to year have fallen far behind inflationary trends. Beginning in 1970 contributions to all United Ways have increased yearly by 2.8, 2.9, 5.8, 6.5, and 6.6 percent. The impact on local units of national organizations is shown by reference to a 1974 survey of the United Way of America. A sample of six national agencies will point up the problem.[6] For the American Red Cross, the income of local units increased by 43 percent from 1970 to 1973, but the income provided by United Ways increased only 6 percent, which as a percentage of total income, declined from 70.3 to 51.9 percent. For the Boy Scouts of America, the total income of local units increased by 35 percent from 1970 to 1974; the percentage of income supplied by United Ways increased 11 percent, and declined as a percent of total from 56.9 to 46.7. Total income for the Arthritis Foundation increased by 19 percent from 1970 to 1973; income from United Ways remained about the same, and as a percentage of total income dropped from 31.3 to 26.3 percent. The trend was the same for Family Service Association of America, where income of local units increased by 26 percent from 1970 to 1974, while United Ways income increased by 6 percent, declining as a percent of total income from 50.6 to 46.5 percent. The comparable figures for the National Association of Mental Health, from 1970 to 1973, were an additional 50 percent total income, with an added 8 percent in United Way income, but declining from 58.1 to 42.7 as a percent of total income. The YMCA report is the same: total income from 1970 to 1973 up 13 percent; United Way income up 10 percent; and a decline from 16 to 15.6 percent in United Way income as a percent of the total.

What these figures in the aggregate suggest is that local units of national organizations have had to find alternative sources of revenue to the United Ways in their communities, but this must be done within United Way rules, which preclude independent campaigns and encourage government contracts. How much worse for the local organization totally dependent on United Way allocations when these are cut back!

But there are forces other than money pressures which are compounding the problems of all voluntary organizations. One of these is the sheer increase in population, and the continued movement of population to urban areas. It is interesting to note that all except six of the first twenty-five Standard Metropolitan Statistical Areas increased in population from 1970 to 1972, and that all of the next twenty-five areas without exception increased in population, some substantially, even though for the country as a whole increases in population were slightly over 1 percent. However, the Bureau of the Census estimates that total population will increase by 2.4 percent from 1972 to 1975, by 5 percent from 1975 to 1980, and by 9.4 percent from 1980 to 1990.[7]

Principally in response to criticism during the 1960s that voluntary agencies were not serving poor persons, disadvantaged persons, and minorities in proportion to their numbers in the community, strenuous efforts were made to take services out to where people were, and to encourage wider use of services. Personal service and health agencies established district and neighborhood offices, public and private colleges encouraged applications, and state universities experimented with open enrollment. At the same time there was a gradual and desirable shift in societal values, particularly with respect to personal services, which markedly reduced the stigma and sense of failure which often prevented persons from seeking needed help. Concomitantly, the need for personalized and neighborhood services has been increased as the depersonalizing impact of technological change, urbanization, and centralization has been felt.

The past decade has witnessed a phenomenal

growth in the number of agencies competing for the charitable dollar. Neighborhood organizations, self-help groups, ghetto organizations and antipoverty groups encouraged by the federal Office of Economic Opportunity, organizations serving minority and disadvantaged groups, consumer groups, and environmental groups have all rightly sought to influence public policy, to exercise some degree of control over programs and issues affecting them, and to gain support from individuals, foundations, and corporations.

Some observers attribute this proliferation of voluntary organizations to the failure of established organizations to change and adapt their programs to meet current needs. Others regard the phenomenon as representing one of the intrinsic and unique attributes of voluntarism—that individuals are free to band together to do something about a commonly felt need.

Nevertheless, it is a fact that the increase in organizations increases the competition for available funds. As Carl Holman, president of the Urban Coalition, observes: "The same dollars get shifted from plate to plate. First it's the blacks' turn, then Puerto Ricans, Chicanos, peace groups, and ecologists."[8]

How are voluntary organizations coping with the acute money crisis? In the aggregate no one knows. What we have observed probably represents more general patterns. In part, the situation is made more complicated by the fact that boards and staff members of voluntary organizations seem to be eternally optimistic—a positive quality which arises out of convictions about the service the organization seeks to provide. Moreover, because it has always been difficult to raise sufficient money to fund service operations adequately, there is an inherent feeling that the current crisis is more of the same, only perhaps

THE MONEY CRUNCH 161

a little worse, and that tomorrow will be a brighter day. We are far from critical of the commitment which these feelings represent. What concerns us is that they may give rise to temporary solutions which may have long-run negative consequences. It is not easy to take the long view when survival appears to be the immediate question.

Consider some of the things that some voluntary organizations are doing in order to meet their payrolls. A simple thing to do, usually, is to borrow money from the bank for current expenses, in the hope that future increased revenue from other sources will underwrite repayment with interest. For many organizations, this carries the "optimistic" approach to its ultimate limit, although sometimes it is both necessary and prudent to take such a step. It is relevant to note the extent to which hospitals have increased their borrowing for capital construction during the past few years and to speculate on the impact of this indebtedness on hospital costs. According to the annual report of the American Association of Fund-Raising Counsel for 1974, an American Hospital Association survey in 1969 revealed that hospital construction projects were in the amount of $1.25 billion, for which 40 percent of the necessary funds had been borrowed. In 1973 capital projects totalled $2.6 billion, of which 50.8 percent was borrowed, and in 1974 projects amounted to $1.92 billion, of which 61 percent was borrowed. The report notes that "borrowing has become increasingly necessary, although the burden of debt service is often staggering. Nevertheless, many hospitals have had to increase borrowing levels to meet inflation in costs."[9]

Another step which an increasing number of organizations appear to be taking is invasion of capital. Frequently this is a consequence of having contracts with public agencies for provision of services for which funds may be urgently needed to sustain a program while the agency is waiting for government money to arrive or, on the other side of the coin, because government money has been suddenly withdrawn, and the voluntary organization feels an obligation to continue the services, at least during a transition period. Or capital may be invaded to make it possible to maintain current operations. Whatever the reason, this is obviously a drastic step for the organization to take, partly because it irrevocably diminishes an asset which is limited in amount, and partly because exhaustion of the principal reduces current and future income in the form of interest or dividends.

For those organizations having an endowment, a less radical step will be to review the portfolio to determine if it can be made to yield greater current income in preference to holding for long-term growth. If investment counsel advises that this can be prudently done, the board may wish to revise its investment policy.

Beyond these three steps which might be classified as money management, the hard-pressed organization is also taking steps with respect to staffing and service patterns. Doubtless many organizations are attempting to cope with the money problem by reduction of staff. In some cases this may be in the form of outright separations; in others, positions vacated by normal resignations and retirements may not be filled. In other agencies salary increments are foregone, and in especially serious situations, staff may be asked to accept a voluntary reduction in salary. None of these courses is easy or desirable. In the first case, the consequence is a reduction in agency service; in the second case, salary reductions fly in the face of persistent inflation; and in every case, the consequences for staff morale are shattering.

Many organizations are attempting to solve their

staffing problems by increasing use of volunteers. What may appear to be a simple solution, as we have said in an earlier chapter, may create a most complex situation. Given the current philosophical, sexist, legislative, vocational, and economic differences of opinion concerning volunteers, any organization that hopes to alleviate its staff problem by use of volunteers must be sure that its own house is in order. By that we mean it must be acutely aware of the volunteer's own perceptions of his or her needs and role; it must have meaningful and skill- and ability-challenging tasks to perform; and it must be prepared in every way to treat the volunteer on a collegial basis. The day is long since gone when the organization can afford to convey the impression that the volunteer is doing tasks which the professional has neither time nor inclination to perform.

Again, organizations have attempted to offset the effects of the money crunch by increasing fees for service. As we have noted earlier, this is a reasonable step to take, but one which contains some built-in limitations, both in terms of what the traffic will bear and in terms of limits in the amount of revenue which can reasonably be expected from this source. Finally, many organizations are meeting the money crunch by seeking to improve their internal management methods, in order to eliminate unnecessary costs of operation and to thereby increase efficiency and, ultimately, the cost-benefit rate for delivery service. We think this is a sufficiently important and, to some extent, misunderstood subject to consider in more detail in a subsequent chapter.

We come now to the most common, and perhaps the most controversial solution to the voluntary organization's money problems—the obtaining of public money. Because obtaining public money is difficult for many types of philanthropic organizations, we offer our observations derived primarily from experience in the social welfare field; with appropriate modification we believe much of this experience is replicable throughout the entire voluntary sector.

At first glance it seems as if the matter could be considered from the point of view of intent: If an organization receives public money to extend a service in the community, consistent with its basic purposes, and based upon a well-conceived community plan which responds to a demonstrated need, one might assume one set of circumstances. On the other hand, if the organization is engaging in a frenetic series of efforts to get government grants, bending its purposes here and there in order to qualify, and if it depends on the grant money to retain its staff and the overhead to balance its budget, one would have to hypothesize a different set of probable outcomes. However, as one pursues this matter in greater depth it becomes evident that the problems and issues are sufficiently generic to permit ignoring the matter of intent. For one thing, the line, if any, between the two situations is very fine. And even if one concludes that the first hypothetical situation contains no hazards, it may very well be that the first government grant is like the first olive in the bottle—after the first, the rest come easy!

Any discussion of government grants for voluntary agencies reveals a certain schizophrenia within the field. An observer who had recently returned from a United Way meeting in Miami, Florida noted that there were several speeches by prominent laymen on the general theme that if we do not support voluntary services, government will take over! At the same time, professionals were attending workshops on how to get more government money! Perhaps better than anything else, this bespeaks the ambivalence within the field today.

In taking note of the recent shift toward government use and financing of voluntary agencies, Elizabeth Wickenden notes that government, especially the federal government, "is seen as too big, too costly, too bureaucratic, too rigid, too remote, too unresponsive, too monolithic, too unadaptable . . ."[10] This view does not lack for supporters. A recent book by Peter Drucker, *The Age of Discontinuity,* puts forward the proposal that virtually all governmental program functions should be "reprivatized." By this he means that they should be delegated or contracted out to autonomous private or quasi-public organizations. Referring to Drucker, Wickenden observes: "He argues that government is by its very nature unfit for the effective delivery of goods and services and should, therefore, be freed from these burdens to concentrate on a leadership role. This role he compares to that of the conductor of an orchestra, although it is not too clear who pays the musicians and who benefits from their music."[11]

An influential economist, Milton Friedman, advocates reduction of the bureaucratic machinery of government by a heavier reliance on the marketplace transaction. He would, for example, give the parents of every school-age child a voucher with which they might purchase an education for their child wherever they chose.[12] Another trend of thinking is supplied by Pifer in his penetrating essay on "The Non-Governmental Organization at Bay." In this, he notes that government has become so large that it has difficulty commanding the resources of skill necessary for the performance of its tasks. In preference to vastly expanding its own bureaucracy, government must look to the voluntary sector to carry out public purposes.[13]

Against this background, there is the natural desire of government to extend services to people requiring them, and the desperate need of many voluntary organizations for additional resources to provide those very services.

Hence comes the increasing use by government of voluntary agencies to carry out public purposes—largely without conscious planning on either side. There is no central point within government which scans the field and attempts to determine whether the impact of government money on the private sector is for good or for ill. Similarly, there is no central point within the voluntary sector which attempts to predict what the outcome of increasing receipt of government money will be in five years, or ten, or twenty.

We believe some very fundamental issues are raised for voluntary organizations. Can voluntary agencies receive public money and still retain ultimate control over their purposes, policies, budgets, programs, and personnel—all of which are normal attributes of autonomy and independence? In our view, these issues are raised by whatever form public money takes, whether for a demonstration project, purchase of service, subvention for general purposes, or a lump sum for a particular service. There are some salient questions which voluntary agencies must ask:

Will public money adversely affect other forms of support, such as United Way, foundation, or church?

Is the proposed program consistent with the organization's basic purpose?

Would the agency wish to offer the program even if no public money were available?

Will the proposed program divert resources, personnel, effort, or space from activities more central to the organization's purpose?

Will a contract or agreement limit the agency's freedom to an unacceptable degree?[14]

We know of no satisfactory formula for the public-private mix of money which can guarantee that the public and voluntary parties will regard each other as strong and

equal parties to a contract, in the legal sense, and which
will protect the freedom and integrity of each. An observer
is entitled to wonder whether a Protestant voluntary
agency with a budget of one million dollars, all but
$30,000 of which is derived from public funds, is volun-
tary or public? What about the agenda at board meetings?
Under these circumstances what decisions remain for the
board to make? Various formulae of 75 percent or even
100 percent for a reimbursement rate for purchase of care
do not seem to go to the heart of the matter.

Rather, must we not consider potential effects of
government money, both on the voluntary agency and on
the community? One matter that ought to be of concern
is the extent to which receipt of public funds restricts the
ability of a voluntary agency to engage in legislative activity, advocacy, or attempts to influence public policy.
One seasoned observer has concluded that an agency receiving public money to carry out a public purpose runs
a risk in thinking it can behave like a voluntary agency in
seeking social reform when actually some part of its program is ultimately controlled by the power of the purse.[15]
One of us was surprised to hear a voluntary agency executive, with great concern for people and a long record as an
activist in their behalf, say that neither he nor his organization could publicly take a stand on a regressive public
welfare policy adopted by the county authorities, which
directly affected persons served by his agency, because 80
percent of his budget came via the same county authorities! It is our considered opinion that an organization's
freedom and effectiveness to engage in advocacy or social
action will be in inverse proportion to the amount of public funds it receives, even when funds are received under
such benign and contractual arrangements as purchase of
service.

As purchase of care expands, especially in the social welfare field, voluntary agencies will be exposed to a new vocabulary arising out of the contractual nature of the relationship with governmental agencies. Voluntary agencies will need to develop much more sophisticated and objective costing procedures and create very refined standards of quantity and quality of services. These are desirable developments. They are things the voluntary sector might have done already on its own initiative if special funding for the necessary research had been available. In addition, there will be monitoring by public authorities which will tend to evaluate contract performance by outcomes, by specific results, and by goal achievement. Contracts will increasingly require that services be spelled out (not "visits as necessary") with specific detail, description, objective criteria of quantity and quality, and outcomes. The public agency will not be buying x-number of input units of work, but so many completed cases in accordance with a well-defined set of standards. This approach will require adjustment by social workers who are understandably more comfortable with a "methodology" approach as compared to an "outcome" approach, of which we shall have more to say later. Meanwhile, to the extent that voluntary organizations commit themselves to a purchase of program service with public authorities, there will of necessity be vastly increased emphasis on grantsmanship, contract negotiation, the acquisition of management skills, and the development of costing procedures. This orientation becomes doubly important when it is considered that one future funding possibility for United Ways is the purchase of service from member agencies, in contrast to the deficit financing method used at present.

One of the issues which is exposed by purchase-of-service arrangements is that of confidentiality. There are two hazards inherent in purchase of service: What are the individual client's rights with respect to personal privacy, and what is the organization's responsibility to protect those rights? With increased use of automated data systems, and wide interfaces with other systems, what uses may be made of confidential information which is supplied? The conflict in values implicit in this issue is underlined in testimony by the Executive Director of the National Assembly for Social Policy and Development before the Secretary's Advisory Committee on Automated Personal Data Systems on November 15, 1972:

> Here is a voluntary agency which is having a great deal of difficulty balancing revenue and expenses. Contracts for purchase of service are available from governmental agencies. The United Fund, which is responsible for supplying that agency's deficit, is putting a great deal of pressure on that agency to accept a contract. But one of the conditions of the contract is that information with respect to cases served by a voluntary agency should go into a state central computer data bank. Now, what the voluntary agency finds as they pursue this question is that there are no regulations with respect to confidentiality, no definition of confidentiality, and the announced interface of the central state-wide data bank with other systems within the state suggests beyond any question that there could be no preservation of the confidentiality which the voluntary agency itself feels is essential to the provision of its own service.[16]

The dilemma of values is caught up in another executive's comment: "We may have to sacrifice a little confidentiality in exchange for funds to serve hundreds of families who would not otherwise be served." Relatively new concepts of the rights of clients, together with the development of automated personal data systems, have created whole new issues, particularly as purchase of service is extended and as reporting requirements are made more extensive.

The extension of purchase of service will also have interesting potential impacts upon communities. The following excerpt from a memorandum dated April 3, 1975 from the National Assembly of National Voluntary Health and Social Welfare Organizations, Inc., describes the provisions of Title 20, the Social Service Amendments of 1974, as they relate to the use of donated funds:

Use of Donated Private Funds

Under current regulations donated private funds may only be used for claiming federal matching if the funds are transferred to the state and under its administrative control; donated without restrictions, except that a community and a service may be specified by the donor; and do not revert to the donor's facility or use. All of these restrictions appear in the new law, except that the final restriction pertaining to revision does *not* apply if the donor is a nonprofit organization. Therefore under the new law the same nonprofit corporation can now be both the donor and provider of service. This increases the pool from which private funds can be donated and the above described eligibility liberalization broadens the use to which these funds may be applied.[17]

This practice makes for a striking reversal of role. Usually voluntary agencies have been affected by the availability of public monies; now public agencies are dependent upon the willingness of United Ways and other nonprofit organizations to provide local matching (or some part of it) in order to generate an additional 75 percent of federal money, which can then be converted into a service package for the community. Once the total grant is received it becomes, as noted, public money and the public agency is theoretically free to use it in any way it chooses, by contract with any provider of service, whether it be another public agency, a proprietary agency, or a voluntary agency, either United Way or non-United Way.

Some provocative questions are raised. Because it is most likely that the United Way will be a major participant in this matching formula, how will contributors to a United Way feel about this potential diversion of United Way money, possibly to a non-United Way or proprietary organization? Some contributors already feel that their gift is too far removed from the object of their generosity; this arrangement adds still one more step. Will this affect giving in any way, or will givers ask why they should not pay the same money in taxes, and essentially, what's the difference? Does this change the relationship of the United Way to its own member agencies? Presumably its allocation will be less because the total United Way "pie" to be sliced up among its member agencies is reduced by the amount contributed to the matching program. Should this agency be obliged to carry out a "public purpose" in order to survive? In the last analysis, who is determining priorities?

In raising these instrumental questions we realize that the reality is that these matching arrangements make possible important extensions of services which would not otherwise be feasible. Moreover, this kind of service packaging makes possible the inclusion of new, emerging groups and the important services they offer. But the dilemma and the conflict of values implicit throughout any discussion of public and voluntary relationships remains: Does one lean toward immediate delivery of services or toward concern for the potential long-run impact on the services of all voluntary agencies?

Another predictable future development for many communities will be an increase in proprietary agencies. Of course, if one is committed to the concept of consumer choice, then there is need for an expansion of the provider base, in order to be able to offer the client as wide a choice as possible. However, in some communities, voluntary agencies are being told, as purchase of service is extended, that proprietary agencies will take over by default if voluntary agencies do not keep up with demand. Cost comparisons between voluntary agencies and proprietaries are not known because of absence of data. In a major study of purchase of service in California, Wisconsin, and Pennsylvania in 1971 the management consulting firm of Booz Allen & Hamilton concluded that relative efficiency is probably a matter of scale, and that the proprietaries are most competitive when large quantities of service are involved, based on sounder administrative practices and cost control.[18] The report lists the advantages of the proprietaries: capital; continuity; sound management; cost control; accountability; economy of scale; reputation for service; and uniformity in service delivered. Many persons on the voluntary side would assert that these attributes are not the exclusive property of the for-profit sector, and would point out that there are other elements which are also important in the delivery of human services, namely, a commitment to the objectives and values inherent in the service, and a professional accountability and responsibility to those served.

A final outcome of the rapid development of purchase of service will be an accelerated development of planning. Unfortunately, planning under voluntary auspices has an uneven record of achievement, and the trend toward merger of independent voluntary planning agencies with local United Way organizations, which do not represent the total voluntary sector, means that other community-wide planning mechanisms will find their way to center stage. The development of purchase of services will raise issues of what services, as a matter of public policy should be expanded, what services should be reduced, and what services should remain at status quo. Obviously, these decisions should be made in the context of a total delivery system. The Booz Allen & Hamilton study calls for a much more sophisticated application of business methods and techniques to these processes. They propose a master analysis plan linking federal-state-local jurisdictions which would establish methods for control of service quantity and quality, and the creation of management tools (time studies and frequency distribution curves to determine the number of interviews necessary to achieve defined and specific objectives) for providing direction and control to the entire delivery system, including purchase of service.

This planning will be different from that to which many within the voluntary sector are accustomed. It will be done under public, not private, auspices. It will not be citizen controlled, but be management planned by professional management experts, whose judgment and decisions will be based on cost-benefit data and facts with respect to efficiency and economy in the delivery of human services.

We believe that the overdevelopment of purchase of service within an organization or community contains serious hazards. One is the potential problem that may arise from potential discontinuities of service. For the individual organization the volume of public money which it receives should never be so great that the agency could not, at least temporarily, withstand abrupt termination of public money and the attendant dislocations of staff and service. The 1972–1973 period witnessed the most recent impact of discontinuity of federal policy in social services on local communities. Not only was a ceiling of $2.5 billion put on these services in 1972, but three subsequent sets of rules and regulations made a concerted effort to reduce these expenditures to $1.5 billion. This reduction was to be achieved by creating conditions of eligibility which would have denied needed services to thousands of persons. An authoritative study by the American Public Welfare Association, released in 1973, reported that an estimated 3,832,929 people and an estimated expenditure of $1 billion would have been affected had the first draft of the rules and regulations been put into effect. It is no wonder the Department of Health, Education and Welfare received over 250,000 letters of protest!

Although most will agree that New York City is atypical and that its experience cannot be replicated elsewhere, it reveals some trends in the evolution of purchase of service in child care that are meaningful universally. Over a long period of time New York City has utilized voluntary agencies for foster home and institutional care for many children who were a public responsibility. Today, approximately 90 percent of these children are cared for by voluntary agencies. A lawsuit, *Wilder v. Sugarman,* filed in July 1973 against eighty-four defendants, including voluntary agencies of the three major faiths, plus officials of the city and state, has exposed some of the problems which are predictable in overdevelopment of purchase of service. The central issue of the suit is whether religious preference exercised by the agencies results in discrimination against black Protestants.[19] Because of the historic utilization of voluntary agencies New York City has never developed a strong, public program of services for children, and because voluntary agencies can exercise highly selective admission policies while the public authorities have not exercised a sufficient measure of regulation or supervision, the result is a fragmented patchwork system of services, with obvious gaps, and with many children falling between the existing agencies. No one appears to be looking at the community as a whole, and the voluntary agencies are said to be unwilling to cooperate. Solution of this conundrum will require more than the wisdom of Solomon, because the voluntary agencies are available, have the capacity and the capability, and above all, need the revenue: it is reported that the voluntary agencies involved receive anywhere from 70 to 95 percent of their funds from the federal and state governments. The principal moral that we derive from the New York City experience is that purchase of service is not conducive to the development of a comprehensive network of services. At best, it should be regarded as supplementary to a basically strong program of publicly administered child care services.

A report of an inquiry by Felice Davidson Perlmutter into the receipt of public money by a group of voluntary agencies in Pennsylvania presents another view. Among her findings are the following: voluntary agencies tend to accept public money when the goals of both are congruent; receipt of public money frees the agency from the problem of dependent financial relationships on the local level, and enables it to function more autonomously in determining its services and in communal planning;

there is no relationship between the amount of public money accepted and agency policy formulation; the experience of these agencies indicates that an arbitrary limit on the amount of public money an agency can receive is irrelevant; lay participation in the agencies is related to mission, and not to the use of public money; and finally, ongoing functional services are not diluted as a result of the existence of publicly funded projects.[20]

Our own opinion is that voluntary agencies should not hesitate to utilize public money, but should establish careful ground rules in so doing: that the program should be within their existing purposes and objectives; that not over a fixed amount of the organization's gross revenue (for example, between 25 and 40 percent) should be from public funds; and that the contractual relationship should reflect the organization's own policies with respect to confidentiality, provision of service, and monitoring. The main thing is that the voluntary organization enter into the relationship as an equal partner, and not be thrust into a position where its financial needs compel it to become a mere conduit for public money, modifying its purposes to the availability of money, and subjecting itself to the hazards of an always capricious and uncertain flow of public money.

We close this chapter with a somewhat radical suggestion, especially at a time when many executives are evaluated basically on the extent to which they have been able to demonstrate substantial increases in the budgets of their organizations. When all potential sources of funds have been reviewed (including the application of some kind of policy establishing limits on public money to be received), the board of an organization has the responsibility, in our view, of facing the hard fact of constructing a balanced budget, fitted to available income. This can be a difficult and soul-searching task. It may mean a reduction and loss of valued and dedicated staff, and it flies in the face of the fact that many people's needs may not be met.

We may be elucidating the obvious when we state that voluntary agencies have never had responsibility for universal coverage. Another way to state that proposition is to say that a voluntary organization has the responsibility to provide service of the highest possible quality, within the limits of its resources and goals. A narrowing of the program base for an organization may permit it to be even clearer about its mission, and to capitalize on it in the community at large. Thus, even in situations where need is not fully met, the voluntary organization can perhaps be more effective as an advocate for those it cannot serve. One of the unique aspects of voluntarism is its flexibility, its ability to retrench as well as expand, and its responsibility to serve as a gadfly to all of society.

NOTES

1. ALAN PIFER, *The Jeopardy of Private Institutions: Report of the President of the Carnegie Corporation* (New York: Carnegie Corporation, 1970), p. 3.
2. American Association of Fund-Raising Counsel, Inc., *Giving USA* (New York: American Association of Fund-Raising Counsel, Inc., 1971), p. 20.
3. "Editorial," *Institutional Investor,* August 1972.
4. GEORGE P. SHULTZ and WILBUR D. MILLS, as quoted in the American Association of Fund-Raising Counsel's *Bulletin 10, Giving USA,* New York, March 1971, p. 1.
5. Commission on Foundations and Private Philanthropy, PETER G. PETERSON, Chairman, *Foundations, Private Giving and Public Policy* (Chicago: University of Chicago Press, 1970), p. 228.
6. United Way, "Information from the 1974 Survey of National Agencies," 1974, p. 219–230. (Mimeographed.)
7. LAURENCE URDANG, ed., *The Official Associated Press Almanac 1975* (Maplewood N.J.: Hammond Almanac, Inc., 1975), p. 223.
8. Quoted by ERNEST HOLSENDOLPH , in "Social Action Hit by Financial Woes," *The New York Times,* November 7, 1974.
9. American Association of Fund-Raising Counsel, Inc., *Giving USA* (New York: American Association of Fund-Raising Counsel, Inc., 1974), p. 40.
10. ELIZABETH WICKENDEN, "Purchase of Care and Services: Effect on Voluntary Agencies." Paper presented at the First Milwaukee Institute on a Social Welfare Issue of the Day, (Milwaukee: Board of Regents of the University of Wisconsin, 1970), p. 42.
11. Ibid.
12. Quoted in ibid., pp. 42–43.

13. ALAN PIFER, *The Nongovernmental Organization at Bay: Report of the President of the Carnegie Corporation* (New York: Carnegie Corporation, 1966), p. 15.
14. Cf. ELMA PHILLIPSON COLE, "Emerging Roles of Non-Profit Voluntary Agencies in the Purchase of Care and Services in the Health and Welfare Field." Paper presented at the First Milwaukee Institute on a Social Welfare Issue of the Day (Milwaukee: Board of Regents of the University of Wisconsin, 1970), p. 51.
15. BERTRAM M. BECK, *Governmental Contracts with Non-Profit Social Welfare Organizations: The Dilemma of Accountability in Modern Government.* As quoted in Gordon Manser's "Implications of Purchase of Service for Voluntary Agencies," *Social Casework,* 53 (June 1972), p. 337.
16. Testimony by the Executive Director of the National Assembly for Social Policy and Development before the U.S. Department of Health, Education and Welfare, Secretary's Advisory Committee on Automated Personal Data Systems, November 15, 1972.
17. National Assembly of National Voluntary Health and Social Welfare Organizations, Inc., Memorandum, April 3, 1975, to Executives of Member Organizations.
18. BOOZ ALLEN & HAMILTON, *Purchase of Social Service; A Study of the Experience in Three States in Purchase of Service by Contract.* As quoted in Gordon Manser's "Implications of Purchase of Service for Voluntary Agencies," *Social Casework,* 53 (June 1972), p. 338.
19. RICHARD SEVERO, "Church Groups See Danger in Child-Care Bias Lawsuit," *The New York Times,* March 16, 1975, p. 1.
20. FELICE DAVIDSON PERLMUTTER, "Public Funds and Private Agencies," *Child Welfare,* (May 1971), pp. 264–270.

PART III

STRUCTURE AND FUNCTION—
INTERNAL ISSUES
AFFECTING VOLUNTARISM

*Can voluntary organizations meet the test of relevance?
How are they to be accountable and how effective and
efficient instruments for carrying forward objectives consistent with the public good?*

8 ARE VOLUNTARY ORGANIZATIONS MEETING NEEDS?

THE ESTABLISHED TRADITIONAL voluntary philanthropic organizations are not meeting needs if the skeptics and critics are correct. Their voices have been heard from foundation board rooms, from government, from academia, and indeed, from the voluntary sector itself. Their messages have been unmistakable: New problems and issues have outrun the voluntary sector; new modes of organizing to achieve goals of self-help and self-determination have become necessary; and new methods of service delivery, staffing, and participation have been beyond the adaptive ability of the traditional voluntary sector. The most common thread running through these strident calls for reform has been that voluntary agencies are no longer relevant because they are not related to the big problems of the day or moment.

In our view the critics must be taken seriously. Their stature as concerned citizens and scholars justifies a careful hearing, and their observations compel advocates for the established voluntary organizations to test their assumptions concerning goals, roles, and purposes. Among the questions that must be asked is what, if any, is the relationship of established agencies to the host of new organizations which are springing into existence. Must established voluntary organizations make major changes as a condition of survival? Are our assumptions with respect to the essential character of voluntary organizations correct?

In their book *Voluntary Associations, Perspectives*

on the Literature, Smith and Freedman note the following criticisms:

> Voluntary organizations, with few exceptions, tend to become internally non-democratic . . . they tend to become bureaucratic, often characterized by apathy, and tend to become oligarchic in the sense that they are controlled by a few persons. Pluralism conceals an elite which controls its activities . . . such an elite invariably represents the "establishment" and membership in voluntary organizations tends to be class based and is often homogeneous.[1]

In a paper prepared for the National Center for Voluntary Action in late 1974, Pablo Eisenberg, Consultant, Center for Community Change, has this to say:

> Yet others perceive the voluntary sector as a complex system of organizations often irrelevant to the pressing issues of social and economic survival in the 1970's and 1980's. . . . The fossilization of traditional practices is everywhere in evidence. Over the past twenty years hundreds, if not thousands, of new local organizations have been created to deal with such issues as ecology, consumer problems, economic and social self-determination, public interest law, poverty and neighborhood revitalization, yet philanthropy has made little or no provision for these new, vital groups. Many social agencies and volunteer groups continue to serve their clients, old and new, as they have for years, irrespective of changing circumstances and the need for modern

strategies and special skills. Nor have philanthropy and many private organizations demonstrated much interest in and concern for the New
Federalism with its dangerous implications for
responsible democracy at the local level and for
the continued vitality of the voluntary sector.[2]

A study was made by Camille J. Lambert Jr. and
Leah R. Lambert of the effects of funds from the Office of
Economic Opportunity on sixteen voluntary agencies in
Pittsburgh, Pennsylvania, from 1965 to 1967. A précis of
the study makes these observations:

> It was found that the agencies had changed little
> with respect to program emphases, types of cli-
> ents served, and modes of service and that the
> agency board members and voluntary funding
> bodies were resisting change. It is suggested that
> pressure tactics be used and that one of the key
> forces for change be indigenous citizens' groups.
> There are indications in Pittsburgh that without
> the successful involvement of indigenous leaders
> in shaping programs affecting their interests,
> pressure from neighborhoods will mount for the
> financing of citizens' groups apart from the estab-
> lished agencies.[3]

Pifer notes that the Office of Economic Opportunity assumed that

> The job was simply not being done by public and
> private agencies nor, was it thought, could it be;
> they were considered too fragmented in their ap-
> proach and too set in their ways, and they were

also seen as being too middle-class, too white, too paternalistic, and too alien to be acceptable to those who were most deeply mired in the "culture of poverty."[4]

Finally, an exploratory study by Donald M. Traunstein and Richard Steinman concludes that

> . . . . a major motivation for the self-help movement has been to construct an alternative to the bureaucratic and professional model of the human services; an alternative to abstract principles and objective criteria, to specificity of expertise and delimited authority, to effective neutrality and impersonal detachment, to technical qualifications and the hierarchical control structure.[5]

What are the essential characteristics of the voluntary agency? The best conceptualization which has been brought to our attention is that of Wickenden, in a paper prepared for the Milwaukee Institute on Purchase of Care and Services.[6] In this paper she notes four characteristics of the voluntary agency: *origins and motivation*—the voluntary agency is assumed to come into existence by reason of the voluntary action of some individual or group proceeding with the intent to render a service. . . . It is responding to a philanthropic, religious, or social impulse in the first instance; *control and management*—a voluntary agency is assumed to be autonomous and control its own destiny, typically under the direction of an independent governing board; *financing*—the voluntary agency is assumed to be financed by voluntary contributions; *choice of service and beneficiary*—the voluntary agency is assumed to have freedom to choose (and hence to delimit) its own area of service, the character of that service, and the clientele to benefit from that service.

The burden of Wickenden's article is to take particular note of the dilution and modification of these "pure" characteristics as a result of the impact of government through licensing, incorporation, regulation, tax exemption and the deductibility of charitable contributions, the impact of increased reliance upon tax funds and third-party funding mechanisms, and the impact of federated fund raising with the controls which are implicit therein. We agree with her observations. Is there, indeed, an open market and do voluntary organizations have the right to select their program, constituency, and those to be served? Are there reasonable tests of relevancy, and who decides? Is ability to raise money the most reliable measure of need and success?

A categorical answer to the question of whether established voluntary agencies are meeting needs is not possible. One's perception of reality and what is actually happening may be quite different. And the mischief is that at no time or place has there ever been the kind of systematic analysis that would produce a factual basis for generalizations about voluntarism as a whole. If one were to defend established voluntary effort the following observations would, we believe, be germane.

As we have said, a common thread of much criticism has been that voluntary agencies are not responsive to the "big" problems of the day. What are the big problems? Over time, public and governmental perception of priorities, for example, in human services, has shifted. At one time or another during the past fifteen years attention, commitment, and resources have moved from poverty to juvenile delinquency, to mental health, to the aged, to environmentalism, to health (although not necessarily in that order). One suspects that those concerned with public policy have a limited attention span, because the leaps from one concern to another are made long before the first problem is anywhere near solved. Whitney Young once observed, in a meeting dealing with national priorities, that this kind of faddism was a "cop-out" by those who refused to deal with the problem of racism.

Even within any of these areas of concern the same kind of faddism (if we may call it that) is taking place. For example, juvenile delinquency was first considered to be an inherited state, then a product of the family, then considered a function of the environment in which the delinquent lives, and then later it was thought to be a consequence of the gap between opportunities and access to them. Each of these concepts requires a different program emphasis for an organization, a different order of resources, and different qualifications and deployment of staff and volunteers. It is not difficult to understand how a voluntary agency may be faulted as failing to relate to the problem of juvenile delinquency if one depends upon the observer's perception of the problem (and its genesis) at any particular time or place.

These observations emphasize the need for a national social report, defined as a collection of time series describing the quality of life, or the state or condition of well-being of society. For example, social indicators could be developed for the following fields: health and illness; social mobility (opportunity); the physical environment; income and poverty; public order and safety; learning, science, and art; participation and alienation; and congestion and population. Were such data available it would be possible to develop coherent national policy with respect to human services and to formulate priorities within them.

It would be immeasurably useful in decisions both within the public and private spheres. As Mancur Olsen observes:

> The compartmentalization and specialization of modern life and assorted institutional inadequacies mean that societies very often make judgments of profound importance without an awareness of the advantages and disadvantages of different options that social science already can provide. . . .
>
> Programs are often passed and public money spent without the question of what these programs or expenditures would actually accomplish even being asked. There is often no systematic examination of whatever fragments of information exist that might permit a better judgment about whether the programs or expenditures at issue are better than the alternatives. Tradition or even inertia have a lot to say about what programs get financed by the government, or what non-governmental efforts get the benefits of philanthropy. . . . At the level of journalists, voters, or charity givers, the hiatus between what is or could be known and what is taken into account is even wider than it is at the level of the governmental agency.[7]

But despite the problems of faddism and lack of basic data for program decisions and priorities, voluntary agencies are doing more in some problem areas than they are often given credit for. When concern for poverty was clearly the number one national priority and when voluntary organizations were subject to widespread criticism as being disengaged from the problems of the poor, the Office of Economic Opportunity funded a study, conducted by

Griffenhagen-Kroeger, Inc. of San Francisco, of nonfederal antipoverty programs in the United States. Thirty-one national voluntary organizations reported, for their prior fiscal year, expenditures for the poor of $2,447,985,000 which was 25.7 percent of their total expenditures. This expenditure of nearly 2.5 billion dollars had allocated somewhat more than one billion dollars for education, including literacy education, remedial education, adult education, and programs for school dropouts. A total of 17.3 percent was spent for health services.[8]

Another comprehensive study bears on this same issue. A study in 1964 by Greenleigh Associates, Inc. of 2,081 families living in blighted, substandard housing in Detroit, Michigan, disclosed that the majority were receiving service from the public welfare department, hospitals and clinics, and the health and social service programs of the schools. However, a total of 10.1 percent reported contact with voluntary agencies, including visiting nurse service, legal aid, family and child welfare agencies, Boy and Girl Scouts, YM and YWCAs, Catholic Youth Organizations, and other neighborhood groups. The report went on to note that there were numerous people with problems who did not seek help and hypothesized that there were three primary reasons: they were not aware of an existing service; they did not recognize the problem or the need for the service; or they considered that the service was too expensive. These reasons appeared to apply particularly to those with mental health problems, family and marital problems, physical and dental problems, those needing day care, and those with legal problems, many of which are provided for under voluntary auspices.[9]

A final insight in this area is supplied by a monumental study released in 1973 by the Family Service Association of America, titled *Progress on Family Problems, A*

Nationwide Study of Clients' and Counselors' Views on Family Agency Services. The research design was intended to supply answers to the following questions (among others): Who comes to family agencies? What problems do clients bring? What services do clients receive? What are the outcomes? A total of 266 member agencies of Family Service Association participated, producing a sample of 3,596 cases served during 1970. We will have occasion to return to this study, but for the moment the following findings are of particular interest:

> These findings undoubtedly reflect the results of agency outreach efforts and the extensive program innovations during the decade. They run counter to the trends that would have been anticipated from the comments of certain critics of the field. For example, Professor Cloward asserted in the early 1960's that there had been "a general disengagement from the poor by private social agencies" and that the "private agency . . . now exists chiefly to serve middle-class people." Similarly, Herman Levin predicted in 1963 that "the voluntary family and children's service agency is heading for a future of progressive specialization and that this specialization will lead to an increasingly refined casework service offered to people of increasingly higher income levels." This prediction is definitely not borne out by the trends in family agency service in the decade of the sixties. The movement has been clearly in the opposite direction.[10]

In our view the findings of these three studies should give pause to those who are inclined toward the sweeping generalization that voluntary agencies do not serve the poor. These are impressive records of service in areas which, by any criteria, are acknowledged as a public responsibility.

What of the indirect impact on the "big" problems? For example, the purpose of the Young Women's Christian Association includes its One Imperative—to thrust its collective power toward the elimination of racism, wherever it exists and by whatever means necessary. In addition, the YWCA has established as targets the eradication of sexism, the empowerment of youth by responding to the self-determination of teens, students, and young women in decision-making and leadership, to advance peace with justice, greater social and economic justice, and a more humane environment. If one were constructing a program to *prevent* juvenile delinquency it would be difficult to improve on these program targets or objectives. Yet one does not immediately associate the YWCA (or any other of the youth-serving agencies) with service to juvenile delinquents. In another area of prevention, the educational programs of several of the national health agencies, such as heart, cancer, and lung have had a positive effect on the health of the nation in sparking earlier detection and treatment of these diseases.

Additional examples of what we mean can be seen in the avowed purpose of Family Service Association of America which is to strengthen family life and serve families under stress. This is done by programs emphasizing counseling, family life education, and advocacy—the latter defined as an action program aimed at insuring that the systems and institutions with direct bearing on families operate to meet effectively the needs and interests of those who use them. Yet it is fair to say that few persons connect these programs directly with such "big" problems as mental health, juvenile delinquency, or the aging. Again, the

National Council of Homemaker-Home Health Aide Services, Inc., describes the essence of its service as maintaining, strengthening, and safeguarding family life. Originally organized to serve children, it has broadened its scope to include many economically, physically and emotionally disadvantaged groups of both children and adults. Indeed, it is likely that this field of service will see a phenomenal growth in the next decade in supplementing professional health services through provision of necessary personal care in the home for individuals during their physical and mental rehabilitative processes, through care of convalescents and those suffering from chronic illness. Yet in the minds of many, Homemaker-Home Health Aide Services is not associated with such "big" problems as the aged, mental illness, or health generally.

The "big" problems, we believe, are problems whose solutions call for the injection of massive public resources, preferably responsive to some assessment of the extent of the problem, and answering to some predetermined set of priorities. That the services of voluntary agencies are ancillary to this concept of public responsibility should in no way denigrate or downgrade their usefulness or importance. Well administered voluntary services can stand or fall by the wayside on their own merits.

If, as these samples show, established organizations are rationally related to some of the major problems of the day, at what are the critics pointing? We believe the most serious criticism of established voluntary organizations is the serious lag in programmatic recognition of the changing character of society and the particular needs which this has evoked. Much of what we mean can be subsumed under the revolution in human rights and expectations which has taken place in the past two decades: the enfranchisement of the poor; the elimination of racism; the self-determination of youth and the aging; the transfer and transformation of power; the emergence of consumerism; the women's liberation movement and the eradication of sexism; and the right of all to participate in those decisions affecting their lives. The adaptation of established organizations to these forces has been, for the most part ponderous, slow, and lacking in effectiveness. Significant efforts have not been launched to reach out and build bridges to special groups; the doors of organizations may be open, but the "welcome mat" has not been visible, and dialogue, communication, and collaboration have been conspicuous by absence. The implications of "working with" rather than "working for" are just beginning to be felt. Nor have there been any noticeable efforts on the part of established organizations to serve as advocates on behalf of the newer emerging groups and their particular interests. The efforts to establish advocacy programs in the local affiliates of one national voluntary organization known to us have been met with every possible reaction from "agreements in principle" and active programs to apathy, disinterest, and opposition. Progress to date has been far out of proportion to what is called for. Is it any wonder then that there has been a veritable explosion of new organizations formed within the past decade in response to concerns within the areas of consumerism, environment, public interest law groups, self-help organizations, neighborhood groups, and the like?

In an effort to understand this phenomenon better, Traunstein and Steinman studied self-help organizations in Albany, New York. The extent of this phenomenon of growth is indicated by the fact that there are now 110 identifiable self-help organizations, almost half of which were formed during the two years preceding the study, compared to 100 of the more traditional health and welfare agencies. Traunstein and Steinman observe:

. . . complex organizations can be typed on the basis of who their prime beneficiaries are (Blau and Scott, 1963)

The Blau-Scott Typology
of Formal Organizations

Type of Organization	Governed by	Prime Beneficiary
Business	Owner	Owner
Commonweal	Voter	Voter
Mutual Benefit	Member	Member
Human Service	Community	Client

And on the basis of this typology they derive certain conclusions for voluntary organizations:

This chart dramatizes the powerlessness of prime beneficiaries of service organizations to influence the policies by which they will be served, in contrast to those of all other types of organizations. The central fact which separates the service organization client from the other three prime beneficiaries: no matter how relatively powerless the latter may be most of the time, or how brainwashed by administrators, they do exist as constitutional entities within the governing structure of each of their organizations. In contrast, the constitutions of human service organizations recognize clients only as beneficiaries. Governed by community influentials and staffed by professionals human service organizations provide clients no role in policy making. . . . The foregoing rationale leads to the following hypothesis: There is a strong tendency for self-help organizations to substitute solidarity and autonomy of members

which are major attributes of mutual benefit associations for professionalism and bureaucratiza-
tion, two major attributes of human service organizations.[11]

We no not mean to imply that all of these new
organizations have been formed as an outcome of failures
on the part of established organizations. Many have goals
and objectives which set them apart from existing organizations; but others have purposes which are sufficiently
congruent with those of established organizations to raise
the question of why some established agency did not see
that need and do something about it, or why, once the
indigenous group is formed, it is not more closely related
to an established organization. We say this with recognition that the development of any voluntary organization,
arising as it does out of the common concerns of its participants, represents the unfolding of voluntarism at its best.
Nevertheless, the failure of established organizations to
adapt their programs and services to the needs of emerging groups and their failure to open the doors of the board
room, the membership, and the staff to persons from these
groups, looms large in any attempt to answer the question
of whether voluntary organizations are meeting needs.

Beyond this matter of adaptability, there are other
deficiencies on the part of established voluntary agencies
which constrict their ability to meet changing and emerging needs.

The first is the reluctance of many organizations to
coordinate services with those of other organizations.
Looking again to the health and welfare fields, social research in the past two or three decades has established that
many families have multiple problems, that these are in-
terdependent phenomena, and require interdisciplinary

solutions. Problems of moving people, of adoption, of poverty, of unemployment, of conflict with the law, to cite just five, require delicate, sensitive, and effective systems of coordinated service to deal with them. A full range of services needs to be orchestrated to serve the family adequately.

And yet it is our impression that the concerted services concept has made very little real headway. Rhetoric has exceeded real accomplishments. The reason is not hard to find. Effective concerted action involves some yielding of autonomy over service and policy decisions to some outside individual or group, and this strikes at the heart of the organization's corporate psyche. Most organizations would prefer to "go it alone," to take credit for, rather than share accomplishments, and would prefer to make their own ground rules for cooperation with others. Concerted action efforts which have been successful have occurred in those instances where agency representatives have formed a consortium for service purposes, and where one organization or individual has served as quarterback, with responsibility for deploying and terminating various organizational services as needed.

This process requires a significant measure of trust and commitment to outcome among both professionals and volunteers. And it will work most successfully when there is some external force which convenes and lends some sanction to the group. One of the most difficult lessons for organizations to learn is that "peers cannot coordinate peers." It is impossible for one organization in an affinity group with similar concerns and objectives to convene the group and assume a coordinating role. Thus the prime elements needed for successful concert of services are some outside organization to start the process and lend a benign sanction over time, and a clear commitment of cooperation from participating organizations. Model cities agencies, comprehensive health planning agencies, community planning councils, and United Ways exist, among others, to provide the former, but a real measure of individual organizational commitment to the broader good is too often missing.

These strong impulses toward autonomy and individualism are also evident in planning processes, whether under public or voluntary auspices. Since planning ultimately tends to influence in some degree the allocation of resources, the relationship of individual organizations to the process is generally not one of cooperation and flexibility aimed at finding what is the common good, but that of a vested interest, resolved to find how the particular allocation will inure to the organization's own benefit. The thought that any particular service is not more important than (or at least equal to) any other service tends to restrict the agenda and the scope of discussion. It may be that public planning agencies will, in the long run, be more successful because of their linkages with those responsible for the allocation of money; but planning under voluntary auspices tends to be successful only as there are volunteers whose influence can be felt around the planning table. This is not to fault agency representatives out of hand. They can and should defend their programs and accomplishments, and if they do not have a deep dedication and commitment to their organization and its purposes, they should not be associated with the organization. What is called for, in our view, is a delicate balance between self-interest of the organization and the broader interests of the community.

Are voluntary organizations meeting needs? We eschew a simplistic response. In general, established voluntary organizations are meeting needs, ranging on some scale from very important to less important. But many have not gone "the second mile" in adaptation to the new demands of today. The emerging groups are, by definition, meeting needs. Their continuation, before they too become established and institutionalized, will depend upon how well they continue to meet the felt needs of their constituencies. As established organizations fail to respond to current needs in the open market of services they will fade from the scene and be replaced by those organizations that do respond. This is as it should be, because voluntarism must continue to be an ever-changing, dynamic, volatile force within American society, or it too will pass from the scene.

Phrasing the problem another way, Pifer, at the annual meeting of the National Assembly of Voluntary Health and Social Welfare Organizations on October 29, 1974 posed a series of questions in response to the query "Is philanthropy serving the public interest well?" *Who benefits? Does it have a redistributive effect? Does it serve people who lack power? Is philanthropy playing a proper role in public policy development?* These are provocative questions, but perhaps of even greater interest is his assumption that voluntary philanthropy should serve the public interest—not alone the private interests of those who may have established or who may now control the organization. This concept of public interest represents the single most significant departure from the "pure" criteria of voluntary organizations, as they have emerged historically. As Wickenden noted, processes of incorporation, licensing, regulation, tax concessions, and the broadening of the potential base of financial support for almost all voluntary organizations have brought about this dramatic change.

Thus the philanthropic organization must function, and permit its relevance to be tested by the extent to which it serves not only the private but also the public interest. And in this instance the criteria are, as Pifer suggests, related to who benefits, how the organization is related to people who lack power, and what the organization's role is in advocacy and social reform. In the last analysis, the public interest will be reflected by the decisions of contributors and of budget and allocations committees, and by the actions of regulatory agencies. Perhaps one test, then, will be found in the public market place.

NOTES

1. Constance Smith and Anne Freedman, *Voluntary Associations: Perspectives on the Literature* (Cambridge: Harvard University Press, 1972), pp. 69–70.
2. Pablo Eisenberg, "The Voluntary Sector: Problems and Challenges" (Paper prepared for the National Center for Voluntary Action, Washington, D.C., 1974), p. 1.
3. Camille J. Lambert, Jr. and Leah R. Lambert, "Impact of Poverty Funds on Voluntary Agencies," *Social Work,* XV (April 1970), p. 53.
4. Alan Pifer, *Annual Report, Carnegie Corporation of New York, 1967.* As quoted in Bertram M. Beck's "The Voluntary Social Welfare Agency: A Reassessment," *Social Science Review,* June 1970, p. 147.
5. Donald M. Traunstein and Richard Steinman, "Voluntary Self-help Organizations: An Exploratory Study," *Journal of Voluntary Action Research,* 2 (October 1973), p. 232.
6. Elizabeth Wickenden, "Purchase of Care and Services: Effect on Voluntary Agencies." Paper presented at the First Milwaukee Institute on a Social Welfare Issue of the Day (Milwaukee: Board of Regents of the University of Wisconsin, 1970), pp. 40–41.
7. Mancur Olsen, "Report on the Feasibility and Organization of a Private Social Report." (Paper presented to the National Assembly for Social Policy and Development, Inc., New York, New York, October 6, 1972), pp. 5–6.
8. Griffenhagen-Kroeger, Inc., *Non-Federal Anti-Poverty Programs in the United States.* Report prepared for the Office of Economic Opportunity, Executive Office of the President, San Francisco, California, July 1965, p. 7.
9. Greenleigh Associates, Inc., *Home Interview Study of Low-Income Households in Detroit, Michigan.* Report of

the study conducted by Greenleigh Associates, Inc., New York, February 1965, p. 95.

10. DOROTHY FAHS BECK and MARY ANN JONES, *Progress on Family Problems* (New York: Family Service Association of America, 1973), p. 3.

11. DONALD M. TRAUNSTEIN and RICHARD STEINMAN, op. cit., p. 232.

9 EFFICIENCY AND THE ECONOMY MYSTIQUE

WE HAVE THUS TITLED this chapter not because we are against efficiency and economy but because we want to emphasize the fallacy of the assumption that business methods of costing and cost-benefit analysis can be directly transferred to the nonprofit sector. To do the latter is to put primary emphasis on economy of operations (low cost) and efficiency or effectiveness (cost-benefit ratio). We are thoroughly committed to prudence and thrift in the expenditure of the contributed dollar, but we think a particular set of problems arises when an attempt is made to apply, beyond a certain point, criteria for the operation of business and profit-making enterprises to voluntary organizations.

For one thing, the profit and nonprofit fields are characterized by immeasurable differences in the value systems which pervade each. One field has a profit orientation and motive which emphasizes low unit costs and thinks about efficiency of production, managerial control, marketing strategy, and pricing as means to that end. On the other hand, the nonprofit sector is primarily concerned with the quality of life and thinks about the accessibility of services, unmet needs, the environment in which people live, and, above all, the quality of service. In the one field the guiding motivation is profit; in the other, the guiding motivation is what happens to people. This is not to say that one is venal, the other noble. Both are integral parts of our complex society. But this difference in value systems pervades both fields, and is reflected in such things as qualifications of staff, organization of services, involvement of consumers, and attitude toward money problems. But despite these wide differences the profit and nonprofit sectors do have common interests, do come together at points of program operations, and do have much that each can contribute to the other.

Another reason why there cannot be a simple transposition of experience from one field to the other is because voluntary philanthropy is a labor intensive field. For example, personnel costs in social welfare average about 60 to 65 percent of total costs: in manufacturing the comparable cost is 24 percent. The same ratio of personnel costs holds for all voluntary philanthropy, and for public services as well. A voluntary organization cannot offset increased costs through increased productivity, or automation, or by sloughing off unprofitable services. A recent report of Louis Harris & Associates noted that, because of the labor intensive character of the voluntary philanthropic field, costs, in the main, are beyond control. Certainly, increases in productivity represented a limited hope. As the report asked, "How much more productivity can you get from a professor of physics or from a corps de ballet or from a painting in a museum?" The following humorous treatment of the subject may not be as farfetched as it seems at first glance:

How to Be Efficient, with Fewer Violins

The following is a report of a work study engineer; a specialist in methods engineering, after a visit to a symphony concert at the Royal Festival Hall in London. For considerable periods, the four oboe players had nothing to do. The number should be reduced and the work spread more evenly over the whole of the concert, thus eliminating peaks of activity.

All the twelve violins were playing identical notes. This seems unnecessary duplication. The staff of this section should be drastically cut. If a large volume of sound is required it could be obtained by electronic apparatus.

Much effort was absorbed in the playing of demi-semiquavers. This seems to be unnecessary refinement. It is recommended that all notes should be rounded up to the nearest semiquaver. If this were done it would be possible to use trainees and lower grade operators more extensively.

There seems to be too much repetition of some musical passages. Scores should be drastically pruned. No useful purpose is served by repeating on the horns a passage which has already been handled by the strings. It is estimated that if all redundant passages were eliminated the whole concert time of two hours could be reduced to twenty minutes and there would be no need for intermission. The conductor agrees generally with these recommendations but expressed the opinion that there might be some falling off in box office receipts. In that unlikely event it should be possible to close sections of the auditorium entirely, with a consequential saving of overhead expenses, lighting, attendance, etc. If worse came to worse the whole thing could be abandoned and the public could go to the Albert Hall instead.

Anonymous memorandum circulating in
London, 1955

The problems of evaluating effectiveness by outcome in the nonprofit field are exceedingly complex. There is little or no scientific evidence of effectiveness, for example, in the social welfare field. How can one measure the effectiveness of a friendly visitor to a home-bound isolated aged person? How can one measure the effectiveness of sensitive counseling to a frightened pregnant teen-ager? How can one measure the effectiveness of a training program for a mentally retarded child? How can one measure the effectiveness of the Camp Fire Girls program for a withdrawn, mistrusting ten-year-old? The same kinds of questions can be asked of those within the various specialities of the medical profession, of educators—in fact, of anyone within the voluntary sector. As William McCurdy, Systems and Information Manager for FSAA, has said, the problem with performance expectation is that of translating human services into operationally defined expectations which can, in turn, be measured in actual performance. There is a substantial gap between knowledge and effectiveness.

Beyond the intrinsic, and perhaps insoluble, questions raised above, there are also some practical problems. While uniform standards of accounting have been developed for hospitals and within education, it is only recently that they have been formulated for the social welfare and health fields as a whole. The Uniform Standards of Accounting and Financial Reporting for voluntary health and welfare organizations, revised in 1974 to accommodate generally accepted accounting principles adopted by the American Institute of Certified Public Accountants, make it possible for health and welfare organizations to cost out program activities, and to separate them from costs of fund raising and management. The production of the United Way of America Services Identification System

(UWASIS) in January 1972, represents a beginning attempt to achieve uniform and comparable definitions of human services programs. Altogether six goals, twenty-two service systems, fifty-seven services, and 171 programs are defined.[1] This system represents a significant advance, which will have multiple uses, the most important for our purposes here being that it provides a key to uniform accounting and program budgeting, and that it is essential in developing management-by-objective or cost-benefit procedures.

The next logical step in a cost-benefit system is defining units of service and giving them some weight. Here we enter relatively uncharted waters. The social welfare field provides examples. In family counseling, an interview may be with an individual, with a husband and wife, or with the entire family group, or members of the family may be part of a larger counseling group. In adoption, the interview may be with the prospective adoptive parents, with references, or with the client who is thinking about giving up a child for adoption. In foster care an interview would likely be held with the child, with the child's parents, and with the foster parents. In each of these examples, the problem is to define a basic unit of service and to weigh it for purposes of costing. Definition of a unit of service is, of course, basic to allocation of indirect costs. Time studies are useful, for costing purposes, in smoothing out variation in times spent on different activities by aggregating experience.

So, while progress can be made in gross costing of services, the correlation of service and outcome represents almost insurmountable obstacles because of the fact that the quality of service, i.e., the professional skill applied, may bear no correlation to outcome. For the medical profession, the patient may get worse, and die; for the social worker, the foster child may run away; for the psychiatrist, the patient may become more depressed; for the teacher, the child may refuse to learn; and for the orchestral conductor, the audience may decline to applaud. Of course, it is also true that a business may go bankrupt despite the best managerial skills that can be applied, and at this point the business manager and the professional have much in common—they want to know why they were not successful. Each will have cogent reasons why they want the answer, but one of the most powerful incentives on the voluntary side is the knowledge that failure has been costly in human terms.

Not only is the voluntary sector motivated by its feeling of responsibility to those served. Increasingly, purchase of service contracts call for payments for service, not "as needed," but as units of input in relation to a determined goal. In addition, in a time of severe money crunch, which seems to be always, funding and allocations bodies are more likely to accord high priority to those services where objectives are presumed to have been achieved. And finally, all organizations are becoming increasingly aware of the fact that they are simultaneously accountable in several directions. These forces lead organizations to pursue efforts to bridge the gap between service and outcome. It is an area in which research is necessary, but research on the scale needed is complex, costly, and time consuming. The essential problem is well stated by Alexander Solzhenitsyn, in his Nobel Prize acceptance speech:

> There are at least several scales of values in the world: one for evaluating events near at hand, another for events far away; aging societies pos-

sess one, young societies another; successful people one, unsuccessful people yet another. The divergent scales of values scream in discordance, they dazzle and daze us, and to avoid the pain, we wave aside all other values but our own.[2]

We do not presume to be familiar with more than a small part of the research that is being done. One illustration comes out of the mental health field. Special Monograph Number 1, of *Evaluation,* November 1973 reports four methods of IGA (Individual Goal Attainment). These are systematic efforts to be more specific with respect to goals than "socialization and if possible, vocational rehabilitation" or "to increase self-confidence" and to be more concrete in regard to goal attainment than "this patient has been doing better, he is more confident, but he is still too rigid—we still have to loosen up his super-ego." These four methods of experimentation range from the simple and concrete to the very complex, involving the use of computers. A measure of success is recorded for each experiment and optimism is voiced with respect to the potential for replication in other settings. At the same time the monograph contains two important reservations. The first is stated by Thomas Kiresuk:

> All of this work is new and exciting, involving considerable ingenuity. All of it, however, has not been around long enough to have received the kind of cautious, thorough, critical peer review that is necessary to understand the work in the context of psychological measurement and to determine the optimal applications that can be made.[3]

The hazard of "survival" as a motive for evaluation is described by Dr. Howard R. Davis:

> What seems to be most often stressed these days as a need for attainment evaluation is to demonstrate program worth—to supporters. As understandable as that motivation is . . . it remains risky. In the first place, evaluations created to show worth have a way of leaning toward that bias. Conversely, evaluations are not subject to the common use of substantiating positions long-since taken.[4]

These caveats lead us to conclude that demonstrated research connecting service and outcome in the human service field may be some time away. Meanwhile, we are impressed with two other methods of evaluating effectiveness and outcome: client evaluation and peer review.

As previously mentioned, *Progress on Family Problems,* released in 1973, examined 3,596 cases. The significant part of this study in the present context was the new approach developed especially for the study—a change score based on a composite of ratings of outcome by counselors and clients in several component areas. The change score, therefore, represents change as perceived by those closest to the treatment process—the client and the counselor. Without going into the rigorous research design which was used, it is interesting to note that evaluations were on the positive side, and that clients tended to respond more positively than did counselors, who tended to a somewhat more modest evaluation of outcome. On the matter of utilizing client judgment the report has this to say:

The findings of the present study also suggests that clients are an indispensable resource for the assessment of service outcomes. Not only do they know considerably more than their counselors about the total range of changes that have occurred, but they also evaluate these changes from their own rather than the agency's perspective. . . .

Clients also have other assets as reporters of change. Clearly, they are a better resource than counselors for information on changes in family members not seen by the counselor, changes in problems or family relationships not directly discussed, and the influence of factors other than agency service. . . .

Therefore, if one had to choose between clients and counselors as reporters of change, present findings would favor reliance on clients.[5]

While we believe this research opens whole new vistas in respect to the matter of determining service outcomes, we must caution that it is not a methodology that can be casually applied. As the authors of the original report state,

A client follow-up study is a substantial undertaking requiring careful advance planning if it is to be successful and productive.[6]

Another impressive method of attempting to correlate services and outcome is accomplished through peer review processes. While this assesses outcome only indirectly, it is nonetheless an appropriate method of achieving accountability in those situations where a high degree of professional skill and judgment is called for.

Within the medical field the PSROs (Professional Standard Review Organizations), established by federal law, are a case in point. The purpose of PSRO is to establish a mechanism for assuring quality of care in Medicaid, Medicare and Child Health Services, all major federally funded health care programs. In order to carry this purpose out an organizational entity has been created in most states under the auspices of the state medical society. It is anticipated that, over time, one effect of this peer review process will be to reduce occupancy levels in acute care facilities substantially.

A good example of the application of this same process within the social welfare field is to be found in the experience of Family and Child Service of Metropolitan Seattle (Washington). The executive, Joseph H. Kahle, describes a pyramidal-collegial administrative structure which he has installed. Designed to facilitate personal growth of staff and the free flow of ideas through all levels of the organization, the aspect of particular interest is the development of the unit organization structure. Workers' units have, as one of their responsibilities, that of evaluation of the performance of each worker who is a member of the unit. As Kahle notes,

> The effectiveness of the working units depends upon the competence, flexibility, and willingness of each worker to expose his practice and accept the evaluation of his colleagues. Two factors are vital to the successful functioning of the unit: respect for each worker as an individual and trust that criticism and evaluation are practice oriented rather than personally directed.[7]

Thus, the purpose of the unit structure is two-fold: first, to serve as a two-way channel of communication between administration and staff and thereby further more effective management, and second, to serve a peer review function for professional staff.

Of particular interest is the report of evaluation in the Huntsville Community Mental Health Center, Huntsville, Alabama. A three-year evaluation program begun in 1971 was based upon the belief that the effectiveness of mental health practices has not been objectively demonstrated, that accountability is possible only if an empirical approach is employed, and that behavior modification is the approach that most nearly approximates the empirical model. The report of the project notes a significant reduction in admissions to state mental hospitals, a reduction in days spent in jail by mental patients, and a high percent of goal attainment by outpatients. Again, a full description of the research methodology is beyond the scope of this book; however, an important part of the research design calls for monitoring the performance of therapists by their peers. The report describes this as follows:

> Once each month, the service coordinator monitors the therapist's performance with a client either by acting as a co-therapist, by listening to an audio tape of the therapy session, or by viewing a video tape. The objectives for the coordinator are to pinpoint behaviors of the therapist that need to be altered, measure the frequency of such behaviors, develop a program to alter them, and provide the therapist with behavioral feedback.[8]

It should be added that the project contains, in addition to this particular peer review process, a method of evaluating treatment success for each client, determined by a point system derived from the assignment of numerical values to the behaviors to be modified, and a calculation of the percentage of goal attainment achieved.

We have belabored this matter of outcomes because we think people should temper their calls for instant cost-benefit information with an appreciation of some of the intrinsic problems. There should be a wider recognition of the research which has been done, and a willingness to invest more in further research, because a substantial investment in research is necessary to advance the present state of the art. And above all, there should be acceptance of what is being done to achieve accountability: research into client responses; processes of peer review; and finally, improvement in management techniques. We believe that, given the present state of deficiency in correlation between services and outcomes, the well-managed organization should be accorded high marks for accountability, for efficiency and economy, and for quality of service.

Discussion with others of the management skills (or absence of them) will bring out an astonishing array of responses. A not uncommon view is that a certain amount of inefficiency, economic waste, and duplication is one of the necessary costs of freedom of choice and pluralism, and that social values should outweigh efficiency values in meeting the needs of people.

In a conversation with Wallace Fulton, Vice-President, Corporate Communications Division, Equitable Life Assurance Company, reference was made to increasing pressure on voluntary organizations from corporations to do a better job. He observed that corporations now have a better understanding of voluntary agencies, and in their contributions, are less likely to be forgiving of "horrendous" management practices. We asked what some of these practices were. Mr. Fulton was specific: high fundraising costs; poor hiring practices, specifically misusing generalists and specialists; antiquated bookkeeping methods; failure to utilize computers; inability to know what they are going to do and how to go about it (poor planning); and financial "float," i.e., money lying around unused, and not earning interest. These are not capricious observations; they come from a respected and responsible businessman who has reviewed hundreds of proposals for corporate support and who has a long and outstanding career of personal service within the voluntary sector.

A third point of view comes from Peter Drucker, who refers in his book, *Management: Tasks, Responsibilities, Practices,* to the budget as an essential feature of the service organization and says:

> Results in a budget based institution mean a larger budget. Performance is the ability to maintain or to increase one's budget.[9]

The point is frequently made that government is much more efficient than the voluntary sector in respect to cost-benefit ratios, allocations processes, and so on. One can wonder if efficiency is served in the reorganization of the Social and Rehabilitation Service of the Department of Health, Education and Welfare, which took place in January 1974. An organization chart of SRS before reorganization contained thirteen squares denoting divisions, offices, and positions. After the reorganization the same chart depicted thirty-three such squares! We must also question vigorously the assumption that governmental budget processes with their trade-offs, political pressures, and response syndromes, are more efficient than citizen review panels of the United Way or Jewish Federations, among other voluntary groups.

It is apparent that the management capability of voluntary organizations runs the scale from excellent to horrendous. Nor can the view that inefficiency is a necessary cost of pluralistic effort be unqualifiedly justified, in our opinion. Organizations may not be able to establish accurate cost-benefit data, but they can strive for efficiency in management. This is an area in which business and voluntary organizations find common ground, and where business can be of help. Among the following subjects may be one on which a voluntary agency executive desperately needs consultation: management by objectives; cost analysis, control, and accountability; computer technology; public relations techniques; information systems technology; purchasing—and on down a long laundry list of subjects upon which a retired executive, a loaned executive, or just informal consultation might prove extremely useful. Initiative must, however, come from the voluntary agency. Businessmen are much too busy to go out looking for public service; moreover, they must be sure the organization really wants help.

An interesting variation of the "loaned executive" concept is taking place in Arizona, where a district court judge, finding five Arizona dairy firm executives guilty of price fixing, sentenced them to make contributions of food, equipment, and services to charitable organizations equal to the fines they faced. The voluntary organizations to which the executives were assigned have been lavish in their praise of the contribution these men are making.[10]

If we are willing to assess an organization by its management capability then we must be ready to apply criteria. We suggest that the following five items are essential and basic components of a good management system:

1. Adherence to established goals, purposes and objectives. This assumes that the organization has gone through a process of establishing, reassessing, and testing what it is in business to do, and that it is attempting to do it.

2. Clear distinction between board (policy) and staff (administrative) roles, and assurance that the participation of board members is enthusiastic and substantive. There are two hazards: an inactive board which may propel an executive into the board's domain of policy; or an overactive board which intervenes in operations. Either can spell the doom of the organization as an efficient operating entity.

3. Internally consistent structure, with clear lines of authority, functions, and delegation. There must be clear and open lines of communication from bottom to top and from top to bottom.

4. Fiscal responsibility. There must be a budget that converts money into program goals, there must be adequate cost controls, and procedures for breaking out expenditures into program services, fund-raising, and management, at a minimum.

5. Practices of full disclosure. The organization must be permeated with the philosophy that it has a responsibility for full disclosure of its operations and expenditures to those to whom the organization is accountable, and to those who may request it. Disclosure is essential to communication with regulatory authorities, and to the various publics served.

Much of what we have been talking about in the last few pages returns to two all-important, interchangeable words—accountability and disclosure. Concepts of accountability are in process of change. Originally, it is probable that voluntary agencies felt largely accountable only to themselves, in that a small group of people founded the organization, funded it, and saw to its operations. But this has gradually changed and today all organizations are accountable in a variety of ways. Not all organizations welcome this change, preferring to operate as tight little systems accountable only to themselves and within the parameters of their own goals and objectives, choosing when and how much their operations should be disclosed to the public. In our view this is a mistake for at least two reasons. In the first place it is only through full disclosure that an organization can really communicate with its publics and with the public generally. And, in the second place, it is only through full disclosure that voluntary organizations can regain that public confidence which has been diminished because of the failure on the part of a few to be honest with the public. All of voluntarism suffers when the executive of an established national agency discloses before a Senate committee that almost half of the money raised by his organization is spent for fund-raising and management, that in addition to his regular salary he gets a substantial "signer's fee," and that only three percent of funds raised by the organization were spent for research, one of its primary purposes according to educational and fund-raising literature. Nor can one understand the comment of a national agency executive in the health and welfare field who claimed that imposition of the Uniform Standards of Accounting and Financial Reporting would "destroy voluntarism" when, in point of fact, the Standards may contribute to the salvation of voluntarism, representing, as they do, a *tour de force* in self-regulation, and in effect saying to the public, "We believe in the importance of full disclosure. . . . We invite your confidence in our operations."

We suggest that a board should look at accountability from five different viewpoints. None of these is new, but they provide a framework for assessment. The first is that the board must be accountable to the purposes of the organization as stated in its articles of incorporation and by-laws. In a way this may sound strange, but we think a board must operate consistently with the purposes which have brought it into being until or unless needs demand change or modification; but such change should be a conscious process, carefully deliberated—not something done at the whim of an executive's preference, or because it will open pursestrings, or for any capricious reason. The second level of accountability is to those persons served. The next is to particular funding sources, such as a United Way, a public agency, third-party payers, and so on. The fourth line of accountability extends to regulatory agencies, local or state. The final line of accountability is to the general public. It is in this last area that an agency's practice may be less clear, but the question of responsibility is not. There are legal and other forces that are compelling. For one, an organization is incorporated by and within a state—hence its very existence is a matter for public acquiescence. It then achieves tax exemption, and contributions to it are tax deductible—each of which are public decisions which impose a certain kind of accountability on the organizations benefitting from those decisions. And finally, the organization may itself conduct a public appeal for money, perhaps for a capital campaign, or may receive money from a United Way, which itself has conducted a public campaign. So there is no way to avoid a measure of public accountability. The principle is clear beyond doubt.

The United Way of America produced an in-house document entitled *House of Accountability*, which attempted to conceptualize and create a model for accountability.[11] It stresses the importance of full disclosure, public reporting, and honest self-evaluation. *House of Accountability* includes service definitions, standards of excellence (what United Way agencies ought to be like), priorities, plans and policies, an accounting manual, a budget and allocations manual, needs delineation methods, and effectiveness assessment methods. The significance of this document lies in the fact that it outlines a base for public accountability which must exist within the total operations of the organization. An organization is not fully accountable when it merely reports statistics on services or data on expenditure. For an organization to be fully accountable it must meet at least the five criteria which we listed above as representing acceptable methods of management. In this sense, accountability becomes an ultimate goal of the organization.

NOTES

1. United Way of America Services Identification System, *People and Programs Need Uniform and Comparable Definitions* . . . (Alexandria, Virginia: United Way of America, 1972).

2. ALEXANDER SOLZHENITSYN. As quoted in Thomas J. Kiresuk's "Goal Attainment Scaling at a County Mental Health Service," *Evaluation,* September 14, 1973, p. 13.

3. THOMAS J. KIRESUK, ibid., p. 16.

4. HOWARD R. DAVIS, "Four Ways to Goal Attainment," *Evaluation,* September 14, 1973, p. 27.

5. DOROTHY FAHS BECK and MARY ANN JONES, *Progress on Family Problems* (New York: Family Service Association of America, 1973), p. 11.

6. DOROTHY FAHS BECK and MARY ANN JONES, *How to Conduct a Client Follow-up Study* (New York: Family Service Association of America, 1974), p. 3.

7. JOSEPH H. KAHLE, "Structuring and Administering a Modern Voluntary Agency," *Social Work,* October 1969, p. 24.

8. DAVID C. BOLIN and LAURENCE KIVENS, "Evaluation in a Community Mental Health Center: Huntsville, Alabama," *Evaluation,* 1974, no. 1, p. 31.

9. PETER DRUCKER, *Management: Tasks, Responsibilities, Practices* (New York: Harper and Row, 1974).

10. "Execs Giving Time To Charity," *New York Post,* February 13, 1975.

11. United Way of America, *House of Accountability,* May 21, 1974. (in-house publication.)

CONCLUSION

The final test of voluntarism will be in its ability to adapt and to regenerate itself in order to respond to the changing needs of a dynamic society. What then is the future of voluntarism?

10 THE FUTURE OF VOLUNTARISM

WE ARE CONVINCED that voluntarism will be tested and judged in the future, not by its uneasy and impulsive response to faddism or capricious trends, but by its attainment of a capacity to make responsible decisions to adapt purposes and programs to changing needs, to embrace change, and to reaffirm commitment to its enduring values. The "attainment of a capacity" we call institutional renewal. This term assumes certain principles underlying renewal and some barriers that always seem to stand in its way. But behind all of this is our abiding belief that commitment to renewal as an ongoing process must lie deep within the minds and hearts of voluntary leaders. We must look to individuals who are psychologically secure, who have a keen sense of history, and who are dissatisfied with the present, to give leadership in processes of renewal.

Far too many organizations operate within the principle of "fragmentation and homogeneity" in which persons of similar values and similar convictions about goals and how to reach them tend to cluster together in organizations, while individuals or small groups of individuals of different convictions tend to break away from the parent organization to join or associate in organizations with which they are more comfortable. This is the easy way. It is more difficult to operate within the inclusive principle of "representativeness and diversity" in which participatory democracy is sought as a reality.

Yet it is only by following this difficult path that voluntarism can affirm these fundamental values in our society—that people have a right to enfranchisement, a right to participate in those decisions affecting their lives, and an obligation to contribute to a better quality of life for all. We deeply believe that this is the only way voluntarism is going to survive.

In particular, this charge to effect constant renewal must be laid upon voluntary organizations, the established, the new, and those yet to be formed. They must achieve a more diversified representation of the community on boards and among volunteers; more diversification within staffs and memberships; and greater involvement of client or consumer groups. This is the most certain path to institutional renewal that we know, the surest way to avoid parochialism, to achieve relevancy, and to embrace meaningful change. The process can not always be neat and orderly, but in the long run there will be improved public confidence, improved board, volunteer member, and staff trust, and both the image and reality of ability to adapt to external change. Thus can voluntarism find its own salvation.

Little did Mrs. Rosa Parks realize, when she refused to move to the rear of the bus in Montgomery, Alabama in December 1955 (she said her feet hurt), that the civil rights struggle was thereby joined. Little did she know that her act would lead to a parallel struggle to enfranchise the poor, that both of these movements would find expression in the concept of "maximum feasible participation" contained in the federal antipoverty law, and that these movements would lead to neighborhood groups, to self-help organizations, to the women's movement, and to consumerism as we experience it today. Not that cause and effect have been that clear; but there has been an irresistible confluence of a variety of forces over the past decade to form what is now seen as a movement for human rights.

How one regards progress depends upon where one chooses to look. If one looks back, immense strides have been made in enfranchisement of the poor, in conversion of privileges to rights, and in moving away from elitism. If one looks ahead, it is obvious that much remains to be done. This gap between what has been done and what needs to be done (we might call it the "plus-minus" syndrome) is quite evident in the voluntary sector. Perhaps its failure to do more, to act as a harbinger of the future are vestiges of its origins when it was predominantly a bastion of the elite. But for the moment, board membership and staff composition are becoming more representative, and services are being extended to new groups. One symbol of change is an increasing tendency to regard persons being served by established organizations not as clients or patients, but as consumers. The difference is more than a matter of semantics. The client was regarded as a person the professional did something for, rather than with. The consumer is a person who exercises choice in respect to the service and the provider, and the service is sought as a matter of right.

The idea of "maximum feasible participation of the poor," a requirement of local community action agencies if they were to receive federal antipoverty funds in the 1960s, has meant different things to different people. To some it meant the provision of jobs, especially the utilization of nonprofessionals. To others it meant what S. M. Miller has called sociotherapy, an effort to involve people in projects to assure them that they can do something about their own destinies, and to reduce their feelings of alienation and apathy.[1] In this connection it is worth noting that, for the first time, according to a survey reported by Louis Harris in the *New York Post* of December 6, 1973, a majority of Americans felt alienated and powerless. By comparison with a similar survey conducted in 1966 the results were striking. In 1966 only 29 percent of Americans felt alienated and powerless; in 1973 a total of 55 percent expressed these feelings. The results of specific questions were even more dramatic. In response to the question, "Do you tend to feel that the rich get richer and the poor get poorer?" 45 percent agreed in 1966 and 76 percent in 1973. To the comment "What you think doesn't count anymore," 37 percent agreed in 1966; 61 percent in 1973. Similarly, for the observation "People running the country don't really care what happens to you," the response was that 9 percent agreed in 1966 and 29 percent agreed in 1973.

The concept of maximum feasible participation has also meant other things. To some it has meant a transfer of power, which implies organizing for political power or action. To others it has meant participation in the formulation of policy, which was seen in the 1960s as the development of neighborhood organizations and the development of competence in making decisions.[2] And to yet others, some maximum feasible participation has meant the opportunity to create self-help organizations as vehicles for service delivery.[3]

Whatever one's perception, it is a fact that maximum feasible participation has taken many institutional forms. It has, in fact, represented a transfer of power, whether power be seen as claiming a right, electing a favored candidate, or influencing policy decisions in a neighborhood or national organization. We like Miller's use of the concepts of transfer and of transformation of power:

I would also urge that professionals seek ways of making the transfer of power to those who have

been deprived of it also a road to the transformation of power. It is not just getting a new set of
leaders with different complexions from the old
but of developing new relationships between the
leaders and the led, between the organs of government and the citizens. The issues today of alienation and anger are not only about who is in power
but about the nature of power as well. New claims
for participation are being raised.[4]

Other observers have noted that we live in a constituency culture. An outlet is needed—the far-out alternative is political redress; another option is for voluntary
action. As one person put it, "There will be voluntary
redress or there will be political redress. But there will be
redress!"[5]

The implications of this for voluntary organizations, especially the established philanthropies, are readily
apparent. But how, and to what end should participation
be sought? The following quotation from the magazine
Trustee speaks in part to the issues:

I have been a hospital trustee for 25 years. . . . My
experience has been that, when a board member
is from a minority group, he or she does not
represent the community at large and in fact acts
principally as a conduit to the group he or she
represents. Such board members typically lend
little, if anything, to the day-to-day deliberations
of the board.[6]

This letter raises questions which have vexed and
perplexed nominating committees in recent years. Should
criteria for membership on the board of a voluntary organization be shared convictions in the goals of the organiza-

tion, friendship with other members in some particular area, expertise in some particular area, representation of community groups, amount of money contributed, place of residence (for national organizations), sex, achievement in business or a profession, and so forth? All of these criteria, and others, have been used from time to time.

In part the situation has been complicated by two developments. The first, articulated by sociologists and students of urban growth, is that the traditional pyramidal structure of communities, in which control, decision making, and power tended to be centralized in a relatively few persons, has given way to a dispersal of influence and decision making among several groups, i.e., business, industry, labor, government, the professions, federations of neighborhood groups, colleges or universities, political parties, to name just a few. Thus, an organization seeking "influentials" for board membership cannot proceed in the same way as it may have done formerly.

A second development has been the insistent demand of many formerly excluded groups for participation in those decision-making processes affecting their lives. The poor, the young, members of racial, religious, and ethnic groups, and the aging are among those whose voices are being heard, and to whom, we believe, voluntary organizations must respond at this juncture in history.

How, then, can voluntary organizations best proceed? What criteria should the nominating committee employ? In our opinion, expertise and diversity are two complementary criteria needed by a viably functioning board.

The first of these is essential since if the organization is to survive it must give primary attention to carrying out its purpose wisely and effectively. There are six kinds of expertise which are desirable, even necessary, for a board to function in such manner: administration; funding; personnel; public relations; community relations; and program development.[7] Persons should first be sought who possess these talents.

Having assurance that these skills can be represented on the board, the nominating committee should then utilize such other guidelines as will insure diversity: ratio of men and women; youth; older persons; racial and ethnic groups; consumers of service; representatives of neighborhood groups, labor, business, the professions, and so on.

This formulation thus takes into account the need of boards for both expertise and diversity, two qualities which, in our view, will further the effectiveness and capabilities for built-in regeneration and renewal of the organization. Ideally speaking, these two criteria will be found in one and the same individual, but practically speaking in order to achieve diversity along with expertise one must, in our present transitional phase, take account of the factors noted in order to achieve more than a mere semblance of representativeness.

In his perceptive article referred to above, Miller addresses himself to another aspect of this problem:

Professionalism has grown strong in many fields. Citizen involvement is growing to balance it off. These changes are cyclical, never-ending. Professionalism and citizenship are in a delicate, dialectical balance, shifting from one period to another. They need each other; they resist each other; they grow from each other; one dominates for a while only to wane in favor of the other.

It seems to me that all services in low-income areas should have active boards containing people from the area, no matter how professionalized the activity. For, if I am right, professionalism should seldom be the sole ruler. A major job would be to help the board to be more informed and analytical rather than to exercise professional skills by seducing the board into the ornamental role.[8]

In the immediate future we believe the pendulum will, and should, swing sharply in favor of the citizen.

The issue of client, or consumer representation is closely related to the matter of community representation. It is another aspect of the transformation of power, or the way power is used. Smith, in the article earlier noted, believes that client and consumer involvement, giving them a significant voice in how the organization is run, marks the surest path to making the organization's service relevant to the needs of those it purports to serve. This should be real, not token representation, or mere window dressing. And above all, these people should be made to feel that their opinions are sought, and are considered to be important. Smith summarizes as follows:

We fought a revolution 200 years ago because many felt "taxation without representation is tyranny." Now a different kind of revolution is being fought by client and consumer groups in this country, but over the same implicit problem of representation. . . . Client representatives on the policy bodies of all human service organizations in sufficient numbers to make a real difference is the root of the coming revolution in this part of the voluntary sector.[9]

In this connection one of the problems for all human service agencies has been how to reach the poor.

Outreach, the utilization of neighborhood aides, and the development of neighborhood service centers have all been tried by health and social welfare service organizations with varying degrees of success. A Human Services Monograph from the University of Texas entitled *Delivery of Health Services to the Poor* reports conclusions from a nationwide review of these special projects. Two of their conclusions are especially relevant:

> Projects making the most serious attempt to employ neighborhood people throughout the health care delivery system, and to upgrade them within the system, had higher levels of patient participation than those not utilizing such personnel.
>
> Projects which most seriously attempted to involve consumers in the planning and delivery of services had higher patient participation levels than those which did not consider these variables important enough to report on.[10]

In the preceding pages we have stressed that basic to all aspirations and commitment to renewal of voluntarism is "letting the people in." We move now to consideration of processes of renewal based on our experiences within established health and welfare organizations, with confidence that many of these processes and proposed policies will have replication in other sectors of voluntarism. To permit an orderly exploration of the topic within this context we suggest the following definition of *renewal:*

> a continuous process by which an organization studies societal and community problems, assesses its purposes, goals, structure, and program in relation to those problems, reestablishes goals,

formulates priorities, and makes needed adaptations and changes to enable it to contribute alone or jointly with other organizations to the solution of those problems.

Some parts of this definition deserve note. By the phrase "a continuous process" we mean that renewal is not a one-time effort. In one form or another it should be going on all the time. By starting with a study of societal and community problems outside of the organization's ambit the sights and perceptions of the organization are raised beyond the narrower bounds of those it presently serves. Putting purposes, goals, structure, and program on the line the organization in effect serves notice that it is open to change. This is not seen as a pro forma, superficial whitewash of what is being done now. And putting as one option, for example, the possibility that programs might be conducted jointly with another organization suggests a recognition that there may be other agencies out there with whom joint efforts would have a multiplier effect. In other words, two plus two might conceivably equal six. The definition as a whole connotes a responsible process. Change, simply for its own sake, is as hazardous to the stability and continuity of an organization as parochialism and resistance to change.

Experience suggests that renewal and change do not come easily. They are abetted by external forces, but there must be a special regenerative effort from within the organization. In a recent article, David Horton Smith reports that researchers have looked into the question of why human service organizations, public, proprietary, or voluntary, tend to be unresponsive to client needs. Why are these agencies out of touch with client needs? Why are the persons in need inadequately or poorly served? Smith goes on to say:

> It happens because of what one writer has called the "iron law of oligarchy" and what another called "the bureaucratic imperative." The first part of the explanation refers to the fact that a few leaders tend to be in control of a large number of participants—even in supposedly democratic, volunteer-based groups. The second part of the explanation refers to the fact that these few main leaders usually become much more interested in organizational survival/growth and their own continuation in power than they are interested in the "official" clients and ostensible goals of the organization.[11]

The fact that only a few persons seem to really care about an organization is a phenomenon familiar to all. Even in large communities it is surprising how the same faces seem to turn up with regularity on committees, commissions, and interagency bodies. So often the busy person is the only one who has time! A study of interlocking directorates would doubtless bear out the so-called "iron law of oligarchy."

More needs to be said about the "bureaucratic imperative." This is frequently not a matter of individual survival, but a matter of organizational survival. When a board and executive are bending all of their efforts to find the resources to keep the organization going, the attitude is understandable when the executive says "Don't talk to me about a self-study. We may be out of business by the first of the year!" Apart from the effect of crises is the subtle effect of the day-to-day job upon the executive. For the able executive every day is found to be exhilarating and challenging. There are new situations and problems to face, decisions to be made, meetings to attend, people to see, travel to take, homework to be done. As Kahle observes, the executive in a social agency must be "A professional social worker, an expert office manager, a reasonably adequate accountant, a wizard at public relations, an excellent personnel officer, a topflight planner, a financial go-getter, and a chief executive."[12] It is natural that the executive should concentrate on the day-to-day job. All the while time is subtly escaping with incredible rapidity. Meanwhile, one of the criteria for the success of the executive is that he or she create a stable environment within the organization, one which reduces controversy, anxiety, and uncertainty within board, staff and volunteers. One can reasonably ask, What executive in his or her right mind would wish to substitute the renewal/change syndrome which potentially contains exactly the opposite elements of controversy, anxiety, and uncertainty?

There are at least two other serious barriers to institutional renewal. One is the fact that it is potentially a painful process—for someone. It is difficult to explain to a small group of dedicated board members that the program which they have served selflessly for many years must be phased out to give way to new methods of service. In one particular instance one of us found that, even though there had been a sharing of findings and preliminary discussion of options before the board, when the actual recommendation was made the board was too shocked by the reality to even respond! In another instance the board members urged that a consultant tell them the truth and spare no one's personal feelings. Yet, when findings were discussed with the board, it was apparent that individual board members felt severely threatened.

Findings and recommendations are, more often than not, equally disturbing to staff members, who may be required to accept changed positions or modified responsibilities, or who may be separated during the implementation phase of a change process. The board may indeed have to fire the executive. None of these courses of action is easy, especially if they involve older workers who have given much of their career in service to the organization or to those served.

Another barrier to institutional renewal and change, largely unrecognized, lies in the differential resistance among board, volunteers and staff members. If we were to formulate this as a general rule it would be stated something like this: In general, board members and volunteers tend to accept and welcome change more than staff members; among staff members, the executive will be more receptive to change than the rest of the staff; and, of all groups, the so-called middle echelon will be the most implacably opposed to change. By the middle echelon we mean assistants to the executive, division or department heads, and the like. We do not know why this should be so, but we have seen it operate time and again, frequently completely frustrating the efforts of a well-intentioned executive, especially during the implementation phase of a study. We speculate that the younger middle-echelon person is bound to the status quo because he or she is upward eager and reluctant to initiate change for fear of upsetting or upstaging the executive. Nor does he or she want to acquire a reputation as a radical or a revolutionary. On the other hand the older middle-echelon person may well be too set in his or her ways, and may simply find prospective change too extremely threatening personally. For whatever reason, special attention must be exercised to enable these individuals to participate in renewal processes if change strategies are to be successful.

Can change then really come from within or must it be motivated by forces outside the organization? There is some evidence to support the latter view. Research conducted by Dr. George W. Fairweather, published in the Fall 1973 issue of *Innovations,* concludes that continuous guidance toward change needs to come not only from the peer group but also from outside change agents. Little or no actual adoption of change occurred even in institutions interested in change when "outside" change agents did not work with the "inside" group. Fairweather notes further that organizations that encouraged more persons and professional groups in the system to participate in decision making were more quickly able to change than those in which decision making was highly controlled at the top.[13]

The National Accreditation Council for Agencies Serving the Blind and Visually Handicapped conducted a survey in 1972 which directly bears on this question. The question raised was whether agencies make improvements in order to qualify for accreditation or to retain accreditation status. Three elements were studied in thirty-two agencies: function and structure; personnel administration and volunteer services; and social services. The findings disclosed that a total of 633 improvements were planned or in progress. After eliminating 12 percent as not being specifically related to a defined standard, the study concentrated on the remaining 557 improvements. The following report of the study is pertinent:

> Improvements were classified under two headings: 1) those that could have been started or implemented long before the agency applied for accreditation—had the agency been motivated to do so; and 2) those that might have been conceived long before but that could not have been implemented without change in outside circumstances independent of accreditation, such as

availability of substantial funds for a new building or additional staff.

Examination of the content of the improvements revealed that by far the greatest number
could have been implemented long before the
agency undertook its self-study, but nothing had
been done until the accredition process stimulated the agency to take action. The conclusions
were consistently supported by statements from
agency staff and board members.[14]

The power of the purse strings is quite possibly the
strongest motivating force in producing change. An example which can be applied to any funding source, public or
voluntary, is the local United Way. The budget or allocations committee regularly sets in motion agency review
processes that frequently result in substantial changes.
These may take the form of modification in purposes,
program, consolidation of services with other agencies,
mergers, or even outright dissolution of an agency. And
it is within the experience of all who have worked in local
communities to observe how change-oriented a local organization can become when the United Way asks for a
study or review! Of course, the opposite is sometimes true,
and organizations may dig in their heels, resist change,
and engage in a show of force with the United Way (which
is sometimes successful).

Our own belief is that, for all voluntary agencies,
the primary regenerative thrust must come from within
the organization. Somewhere, whether it be in members,
board, or staff, there must be a commitment to renewal,
to change, and to relevance. Without this, the influence of
outside forces, whether it be the United Way, a consulting
firm, or a public agency, may be transitory and ineffective

in producing real change. The analogy may not be apt, but one thinks of the country of Sri Lanka (Ceylon). The country was occupied by the Portugese for 100 years, by the Dutch for 100 years, and by the British for 200 years and yet these successive efforts at colonizing and transforming the country have proven futile. Sri Lanka retains today its culture, its values, its customs, and its traditions. We do not know how cultural anthropologists would explain this but it seems evident that the people liked things the way they were and resisted change. It seems safe to predict that when they are ready for change, it will come.

There are a number of things which any organization can do to reflect readiness to change. Some are direct actions, others are indirect in that they help to create a climate conducive to movement and change. All of them can be set in motion with a minimum of fanfare, preparation, or resources. There are two direct activities that look toward renewal. The first is the agency self-study, which should be conducted at least every five years. It should be a formal, comprehensive review of the organization and the community at a given point in time, and should engage members, board, executive, and staff. In addition, every organization should have a formal outside study at least every ten years, utilizing an independent research or consulting firm.

The criteria for selection of a consulting firm should emphasize the firm's willingness to work with, rather than for, members, board, and staff, and the firm's understanding that it is really initiating a process, rather than simply providing the board with a beautifully prepared report, complete with well turned out recommendations. Because any study really compresses into a very short time frame a process that would normally go on all the time, involvement of membership, board and staff at all phases is indispensable. It has been said that the most successful studies are those in which 50 percent of the recommendations have been implemented before the consultant leaves town.

There are "horror stories" in the social welfare field of what happens when studies are done the other way. In one large community an outside study was conducted of the services of several family service agencies. Everyone was in the dark about the consultant's findings and his recommendations. At last his report was received—after he had left town—and it was not difficult to understand why his proposal for a merger of the three large agencies fell on hostile ears. Had he shared his findings with the organizations involved, had he tested readiness to accept his recommendations, had he brought the leadership of the agencies carefully along, it is quite possible that the recommendations would have been accepted. As it was, the consensus was that he had set back a needed reorganization of services by at least ten years! In the last analysis, it is probably true that the process of working on agency goals, purposes, and programs is more important than the specific study recommendations because the process itself tends to engender perspectives and values which reject parochialism and narrowness of viewpoints.

Of course, not all surveys are successful, even if well done, as Smith reminds us:

> But even if the evaluation is well done, the leadership of your organization (you included!) may refuse to accept its implications. Too often the leadership will only accept those findings and recommendations with which they already agree or find convenient to accept.[15]

As he further observes,

> The bureaucratic imperative continues to hold sway and clients' needs are still inadequately met. Alternative self-help organizations grow rapidly. Traditional human service organization budgets, images, and support suffer.[16]

There are other things which any organization intent on creating a climate favorable to renewal can engage in. One is the periodic staff or board retreat which enables staff or board to get away from the pressure of the day-to-day job and to look with a measure of detachment at what is being done and where the organization is going. It is not only a vehicle for "instant refreshment" but also a means of taking the long look ahead. Even the regular staff meeting can contribute toward the same end. Different methods of utilizing staff meetings are familiar to all. At one end of the spectrum stands the executive who utilized occasional staff meetings to announce decisions and to review marching orders for the day. At the other end is the executive who systematically involves his total staff in the affairs of the organization. This model might be called the quasi-collegial model, in which the expertise, experience, and judgment of the staff are sought and taken seriously into account in formulating the options from which the executive must make decisions. And in this same connection it is safe to say that the contribution of staff to this process will bear some relationship to its diversity—diversity of age, background, sex, racial composition, and experience. A staff which is homogeneous will tend to produce homogeneous sets of ideas; a staff which is heterogeneous by these several criteria will, by the interaction of their diverse perceptions, produce a great deal more electricity, and it is this kind of electricity which can generate power and energy for renewal and change.

A key element in this matter of renewal and change is the executive. The first question is, Does the organization have a procedure for periodic review of the executive? Many organizations do, but it is likely that more do not, and that once an executive is on the job he remains there short of malfeasance or because he or she leaves to take another job. Few executives are called to account for nonfeasance, which we think is quite as serious as malfeasance. We think every organization should have a built-in procedure for periodic review of the executive's performance and that there should be a limit on tenure of ten years. While this latter recommendation will be controversial to some, its implementation will make a major contribution to institutional, and to individual renewal, in our judgment. Somewhere between five and ten years on the job, the executive has settled into and knows the job. He or she understands and operates within its parameters, its constraints, and its opportunities. By ten years, the executive will have made his or her major contribution to the job, and the job will have made its major contribution to his or her development. Thus the demands for further individual and organizational growth suggest that it is time to move along. This suggestion does not denigrate any individual's on-the-job performance at ten years. One executive of a voluntary national organization argued that it would be best for the individual and the organization to limit executive tenure to five years, but he never followed his own advice! But this does emphasize the point that there is no indispensable man or woman—and any organization which allows itself to drift into this mode of thinking about anyone, whether it be the executive or a board member, is creating a situation in which change and renewal become more difficult. Big business tends to weed out people and assure turnover by non-promotion. Voluntary agencies need a policy to assure turnover at the top.

We hope we have conveyed the urgency of our views. Only by opening their doors to the rich diversity of all emerging groups as members, volunteers, board, and staff, can voluntary organizations find the spark which will ignite internally generated change. Only by constant regeneration and renewal can voluntarism survive.

NOTES

1. S. M. MILLER, "The Future of Maximum Feasible Participation" (Outline of a paper as presented at the Alumni Conference of the Columbia University School of Social Work, New York, N.Y., May 4, 1968), pp. 1–2.
2. Ibid., p. 1.
3. SANFORD KRAVITZ, "Voluntary Agencies and Their Relationship to Government" (Paper prepared for the 75th Anniversary Assessment Project of the Hudson Guild of New York, February 1971), p. 22.
4. S. M. MILLER, op. cit., pp. 5–6.
5. Interview with Wallace Fulton, Vice-President of Equitable Life Assurance Society, Corporate Communications Division, New York City, January 10, 1975.
6. "On Community Representation," *Trustee,* March 1975, p. 8.
7. The authors are indebted to Joseph Weber, Assistant Director, New York Fund, for this formulation.
8. S. M. MILLER, op. cit., p. 8.
9. DAVID HORTON SMITH, "Research," *Voluntary Action Leadership,* Spring 1975, p. 8.
10. JAMES C. STEWARD and LOTTIE LEE CRAFTON, *Delivery of Health Care Services to the Poor* (Austin: Center for Social Work Research, University of Texas, 1975), pp. 17–18.
11. DAVID HORTON SMITH, op. cit., p. 30.
12. JOSEPH H. KAHLE, "Structuring and Administering a Modern Voluntary Agency," *Social Work,* October 1969, p. 28.
13. GEORGE W. FAIRWEATHER, *Innovations,* Vol. I (Ann Arbor, Michigan: American Institutes for Research, 1973), p. 1.
14. PETER G. MEEK, Consultant, "Self-Regulation in Private

Philanthropy" (Report prepared for the Commission on Private Philanthropy and Public Needs, September 1974), p. 151.

15. DAVID HORTON SMITH, op. cit., p. 30.
16. Ibid.

EPILOGUE

VOLUNTARISM STANDS at the crossroads. We are convinced that its survival will depend upon the interplay of forces both outside and within itself. The outside forces represent necessary governmental policies:

1. A provision in federal tax policy of continuity and encouragement to voluntary giving.
2. The extension and fixing of precise, measurable limits to permissible legislative activity.
3. Policies governing purchase of service which respect the integrity of voluntary organizations as "equal partners" and which recognize the potential negative impact of excessive public funding on the independence of the voluntary organization.
4. Recognition that, while all regulatory activities proceed on the assumption that charity exists for the benefit of the whole community, overkill defeats its constructive purpose.

But the major task that lies ahead belongs to voluntarism—to put its own house in order—else it will not warrant the affirmative governmental policies which are called for here. We find six critical objectives to be met by voluntary bodies:

1. The broad spectrum of organizations which voluntarism comprises must tap and utilize

the rich diversity of individuals who make up our country; enfranchisement and participatory democracy must become a reality.

2. All voluntary organizations must build in policies and processes requiring a periodic review of goals, objectives, purposes, and programs in order to adapt to changing times, conditions, and needs.

3. Within whatever limits may be established by law and regulation, voluntary organizations must substantially increase the commitment of their resources to advocacy, influencing public policy, and contributing to social reform.

4. Organizations must actively seek, recruit, train, and constructively engage more volunteers from the vast reservoir of compassion, altruism, and commitment which exists among all people.

5. Voluntary organizations must remember that they exist by public sanction, that many subsist by public generosity in giving, and that beyond their particular publics, all are ultimately accountable to the general public, and its representatives.

6. Voluntary organizations must constantly see themselves, not as isolated islands of program or service, but as integral parts of a network of service or influence, whose common objectives can be multiplied by participation in consortia, ad hoc coalitions, and concerted arrangements.

Should all voluntary organizations, by a stroke of the pen, translate these principles into active operating policies, and should government, at the same time, resolve to be guided by the four suggested policies, together they would then reflect an affirmative and consistent philosophy about the place, justification, legal status, cultural value, and authentic role of voluntarism in our society.

At the height of the economic upheavals caused by the Great Depression, the economists produced for us the concept of the Gross National Product, which has ever since served as a backbone of economic theory and policy; in the desperate hours of World War II our physicists split the atom and provided the breakthrough that ultimately ended the war; in the late forties and early fifties it was the mathematicians who catapulted us into a computer age; and in the turbulent sixties our country responded to the cries for enfranchisement, equal rights, and opportunity by reaffirming the sanctity of human rights. Can we, the persons who by volunteer or professional involvement are most deeply concerned with the values and goals of this society and their effective implementation in the lives of the persons we serve, fail to respond to the challenge posed by the crisis of voluntarism? Will we give to the generation that is now embarking on a third century of nationhood a legacy of the greatest goals and values this world has ever known, based on the Judeo-Christian heritage, refined to meet the needs of a post-industrial, humanistic society, and made real by the dedicated efforts of professionals and volunteers? Or will we, like the ancient Romans, divide within ourselves, dissipate our energies, and thereby sow the seeds of our own destruction? We are at the crossroads, and the choice of direction is ours.

APPENDIX

COMMENTARY ON THE FILER COMMISSION REPORT

IT WAS JUST as this book was going to press that two very relevant studies were made public: the report of the Commission on Private Philanthropy and Public Needs (the "Filer Report") titled *Giving in America: Toward a Stronger Voluntary Sector,* and the report of the Donee Group titled *Private Philanthropy: Vital and Innovative or Passive and Irrelevant.* The Donee Group, a coalition of public interest, social action, and volunteer groups, was formed as a response to criticism of the Filer Commission that it was too oriented to preservation of the status quo and the "established" organizations, and that it failed to assess changing public needs and give recognition to new forms of voluntary effort.

The two reports, despite their different conclusions and recommendations on several issues, complement each other and need to be read together. As we have said elsewhere, it is our view that if voluntarism is to survive it must preserve the best of what exists, cast off that which is outmoded, and be prepared to embrace new issues, new participants, and new forms of enterprise. We agree with much in each report; we disagree at other points.

We think it was important for the Filer Commission to have emphasized the issues of voluntary giving and tax reform. Present uncertainty with respect to governmental policy has not served the voluntary sector well. It is significant, in the consideration of future public policy, that the Commission stood solidly behind the present system of contribution deductibility, in preference to systems of credits or matching proposals. One of the most important contributions of the Commission's work is to be found in the research of Professor Martin Feldstein, which proved the "efficiency" of giving under present laws—i.e., that the amount of money gained by voluntary organizations is greater than the revenue forgone by the government through tax deductions for charitable contributions. The Commission's recommendation for increasing incentives for low- and middle-income taxpayers by the double and one-and-a-half deduction, to offset the nonincentive inherent in the standard deduction and to ameliorate the inequity in the way the deduction now operates, are worthy of careful study though we wish they had extended this same incentive formula to upper-income brackets. But we thoroughly agree with the concept of public accountability which pervades much of the Commission's report. Voluntary organizations must extend their accountability beyond the traditional limits of boards and contributors.

We wish the Filer Commission had given more attention to the changing situation with respect to volunteers. It is a significant finding that the value of contributed time in the United States ($26 billion) is equal to the value of contributed dollars. Yet this priceless asset of the voluntary sector is undergoing severe strain and its future is uncertain. With the visual acuity of hindsight we also wish the Commission had expended some of its funds in a well-planned series of regional meetings around the country to test its findings and the "drift of its thinking" with the grassroots before committing its conclusions to final recommendations. Whether or how this might have changed its recommendations cannot be known, but it would have afforded different perspectives, different points of view, and a citizen base for implementation of recommendations that can be secured in no other way. So, also, a more continuous liaison with established voluntary organizations would have enriched the Commission's deliberations and provided a core of solid support for the final report.

We disagree with two of the Commission's recommendations. We believe that the audit and ruling functions of the IRS should be removed to a new governmental entity, preferably modeled on the proposal of Alan Pifer, described elsewhere. While we only tentatively agreed with this option six months ago (when that section of the book was written) we now vote for it with enthusiasm. As an outcome of this preference, we disagree with the Commission's recommendation for a new, permanent, quasi-governmental commission. Given the public center, as proposed above, it remains for the voluntary sector itself to provide a vehicle for continuous communication, information, coordination, and such joint projects as might be agreed upon on an ad hoc basis. We do not propose a super organization, which would be contrary to the pluralistic concepts we advance, or a new organization, but simply the better use of those that now exist. This might be done through general agreement to enhance the functions of a single organization, or these objectives might be achieved through a consortium of existing organizations. In either case, it would represent a voluntary solution to a felt need.

One simple fact in regard to the Donee Group is that it exists. When the Hamlin report was issued in 1961 and the Peterson report in 1970 there was no spontaneous reaction from the grassroots. The growth of constituencies which the Donee Group represents (organizations involved in minority rights, urban affairs, tax reform, environmental action, public interest law, and so on) is a relatively recent phenomenon. That these groups have been able to coalesce, to formulate a set of values and recommendations, and to have an impact on the work of the Filer Commission, attests to the vigor of the entire voluntary sector. That the Donee group, with other like-minded organizations, has now formed the Committee for Responsive Philanthropy, a new national organization, to monitor and act as a watchdog in relation to the sector, is assurance that their point of view will continue to be part of the necessary debate of public policy issues in the future.

We agree with the value orientation of the Donee Group, with their point of view concerning accountability, and with many of their recommendations, although we frequently seek the same ends in different ways. As a case in point, we have greater faith than does the Donee Group in regenerative forces within voluntary organizations, as opposed to the necessity of legal means.

We have two additional observations. We think the Donee Group, in some of its criticisms of foundations, does not take sufficiently into account the chilling effect of the Tax Reform Act of 1969 on the freedom, creativity, and willingness of foundations to take risks. Foundations saw the Tax Reform Act of 1969 as, in effect, punishing them for being controversial, innovative, and too liberal. The result was a more conservative posture on the part of all foundations.

Another observation is that the Donee Group does not, in our judgment, sufficiently assess the ultimate impact of government money and accompanying control on the voluntary sector. We realize that sometimes private control can be as onerous as government control, but to implicitly assume, as the Donee Group has seemingly done, that government control is benign and will not ultimately change and perhaps destroy voluntarism as we know it, is a proposition we cannot accept.

In any case, the advent of the Filer and Donee reports is bound to stimulate and enrich the necessary debate that must precede those changes in public policy and private behavior which are so essential to the furtherance of voluntary effort in the next few decades.

INDEX

Action, 43, 48 n. 7., 58, 60, 61
Adams, James Luther, 131, 151
    n. 5.
Ad Hoc Citizen's Committee
    (Hamlin Report), see
    "Voluntary Health and
    Welfare Agencies in the
    United States"
Advisory Commission on Inter-
    governmental Relations,
    91, 92
American Association of Fund-
    Raising Counsel, 42–47, 49
    n. 10., 49 n. 12., 49 n. 15.,
    153, 154, 161, 178 n. 2., 178
    n. 9.
American Cancer Society v.
    City of Dayton, 82
American Heart Association,
    100
American Institute of Certified
    Public Accountants, 95,
    96, 206; Audit Guide, 95,
    105 n. 26., 105 n. 27.; In-
    dustry Audit Guide, 96
American Public Welfare Asso-
    ciation, 174
American Red Cross, 32, 55,
    158
"Americans Volunteer," study
    by the Bureau of the Cen-
    sus for ACTION (U. S.
    Government Agency), 43,
    44, 49 n. 14, 60, 63, 65 n.
    10.

Antipoverty Program (Office of
    Economic   Opportunity),
    33, 35, 160, 185, 186, 189–
    190, 201 n. 8.
Aristotle, 21, 22, 35
Association of Junior Leagues,
    55, 59, 65 n. 12.
Asylum for the Deaf (Hartford,
    Conn.) 31, 32

Baetz, Reuben, 63
Bell, Daniel, 132, 151 n. 6.
Bicentennial, a time to reassess
    voluntarism, 13
Bittker, Boris I., 110, 111, 114,
    115, 124 n. 3., 124 n. 4., 124
    n. 5., 124 n. 6.
Booz Allen and Hamilton, 172,
    173, 179 n. 18.
Borod, Ronald S., "Lobbying
    for the Public Interest,"
    130, 131, 143, 144, 151 n.
    4., 151 n. 9., 151 n. 10., 151
    n. 11.

Call for Action, 59
Canadian Council on Social De-
    velopment,   "Volunteers,
    the Untapped Potential,"
    63, 66 n. 16.
Cantwell v. Connecticut, 81, 82
Carnegie Corporation, Annual
    Report of (1974), 128, 151
    n. 1.; Annual Report of
    (1970), 153, 178 n. 1.; An-

nual Report of (1966), 165, 179 n. 13.; Annual Report of (1967), 201 n. 4.

Carter, Richard, 29, 30, 37 n. 8.

Charitable contributions, tax reform and, 107; as subsidy, 109; elimination of, 111; as consumption expenditure, 114; consistent with equity and progressivity, 113–117; effectiveness of, 117–119; unique quality of, 119, 120; as deduction from gross income, 120–122

Charity, definition of, 40

Charity Organization Society, 28, 32, 54, 56

Chalmers, Reverend Thomas (Scottish Minister), 28

Child Welfare League of America, 93, 100

Class, Norris E., "The Regulatory Challenge to Social Work," 69, 70, 103 n. 2.

Coalition for the Public Good, 42, 116, 122, 124 n. 8.

Cohen, Sheldon, 89, 104 n. 19.

Commission on Foundations and Private Philanthropy (Peterson Commission), see "Foundations, Private Giving and Public Policy"

Commission on Private Philanthropy and Public Needs (Filer Commission), see also, "Giving in America: Toward a Stronger Voluntary Sector," 73, 79, 80, 84, 86, 103 n. 9., 103 n. 13.,

119, 154, 245 n. 14., 251–254.

Committee for Responsive Philanthropy, 253

Conable, Barber B. (U. S. Congressman), 139, 141, 142

Council of Better Business Bureaus, 71, 84, 97–100; "Standards for Charitable Solicitations," 98–100, 105 n. 29.

Daughters of Charity, 27

Davis, Dr. Howard R., 210, 221 n. 4.

"Delivery of Health Services to the Poor," by James C. Steward and Lottie Lee Crafton, 233, 245 n. 10.

Dixon, John, 42

Donee Group Report, "Private Philanthropy: Vital and Innovative or Passive and Irrelevant?" 251–254

Drucker, Peter, "The Age of Discontinuity," 165; "Management: Tasks, Responsibilities, Practices," 215, 221 n. 9.

Dunant, Jean Henri (Swiss Banker), 32

Economy (see Efficiency)

Efficiency, 203–205; evaluating effectiveness, 206–214; client evaluation, 210, 211; peer review, 211–214; management capability, 214–217 accountability and disclosure, 218–220

Eisenberg, Pablo, 184, 185, 201 n. 2.

England, 27–29; Poor Law, 27–29; Law of Charitable Uses, 40; Charity Commissioners, 89, 90; doctrine of parens patriae, 70

"Evaluation," 209, 210, 221 n. 2., 221 n. 3., 221 n. 4., 221 n. 8.

Fairweather, Dr. George W., 238, 245 n. 13.

Family and Child Service of Metropolitan Seattle, 212

Family Service Association of America, 100, 151 n. 13., 158, 190, 191, 202 n. 10., 192, 221 n. 5., 221 n. 6.

Feldstein, Martin, 118, 119, 124 n. 11., 252

Filer Commission, see Commission on Private Philanthropy and Public Needs

501 (C) 3 Group, 49 n. 17., 69, 118–123, 125 n. 14.

"Foundations, Private Giving and Public Policy," 73, 88, 89, 104 n. 18., 117, 124 n. 10., 155–157, 178 n. 5., 253

Francis of Assisi (Saint), 25

Franklin, Benjamin, 30, 31

Freedman, Anne, "Voluntary Associations, Perspectives on the Literature," 183, 184, 201 n. 1.

Fremont-Smith, Marion, 86, 104 n. 14., 104 n. 20.

Frey, Elizabeth, 32

Friedman, Milton, 165

Fulton, Wallace, 214, 215, 245 n. 5.

Germantown School for the Mentally Deficient (Penn.), 32

"Giving in America: Toward a Stronger Voluntary Sector," see also Commission on Private Philanthropy and Public Needs (Filer Commission)

Gospel Army v. Los Angeles, 85, 86

Gracchus, Caius, 21, 22

Gracchus, Tiberius 21, 22

Greenleigh Associates, Inc., 190, 201 n. 9.

Griffenhagen-Kroeger, Inc., 189, 190, 201 n. 8.

Grimes, Arthur J. (Jack), 84, 85, 103 n. 13.

Gunn-Platt Survey of 1945, 73

Hamlin Report, see "Voluntary Health and Welfare Agencies in the United States"

Harris, Louis and Associates, 204, 227, 228

Height, Dorothy, 59

Holman, Carl, 160

Howard, John, 32

Human rights movement, 226.

Hunter, T. Willard, "The Tax Climate for Philanthropy," 117, 124 n. 9.

Huntsville Community Mental Health Center (Alabama), 213, 214, 221 n. 8.

"[The] Impact of the Minimum Distribution Rule on Foundations," Norman D. Ture, 75, 76, 103 n. 5., n. 6.
"Innovation" (Fairweather), 238, 245 n. 13.
Institutional Investor, 154, 178 n. 3.
Institutional renewal, 225; definition of, 233; 234; barriers to 234, 237; readiness to change, 240; agency review, 240, 241, executive performance review, 243
Internal Revenue Code, 40, 45, 62, 66 n. 15., 111, 135–137, 139, 140, 142–146
Internal Revenue Service, 42, 72, 74, 77, 78, 84, 87, 89–91, 111, 137, 139

Johnson, Lyndon B. (President), 33, 34
Joint Committee on Accreditation of Hospitals, 93, 100
Journal of Current Social Issues, 129, 151 n. 2., 151 n. 3., 151 n. 5., 151 n. 12.
Judeo-Christian heritage, 19–28, 35, 117, 249

Kahle, Joseph H., 212, 221 n. 7., 235, 236, 245 n. 12.
Karth, Joseph E. (U. S. Congressman), 76
Kennedy, Robert F., 9
Kiresuk, Thomas J., 209, 221 n. 2., 221 n. 3.

Lambert, Camille J., Jr., 185, 201 n. 3.
Lambert, L. R., 185, 201 n. 3.
League of Women Voters, 55
Levin, Herman, 58, 65 n. 3., 65 n. 6., 65 n. 8., 65 n. 9.

McCurdy, William, 206

Maimonides, 23
Meek, Peter, 79, 80, 92, 93, 103 n. 9., 104 n. 17., 104 n. 23, 245 n. 14.
Miller, S. M., 48 n. 6., 227, 228, 229, 231, 232, 245 n. 1., 245 n. 2., 245 n. 4., 245 n. 8.
Mills, Wilbur, D., 154, 155, 178 n. 4.
Mondale, Walter (U. S. Senator), 76–79, 103 n. 8.
Money problem, 153; impact of inflation on, 155; increased cost of doing business, 155; voluntary services are labor-intensive, 155; how voluntary organizations cope with, 160–163.
Muskie, Edmund (U. S. Senator), 139

National Accreditation Council for Agencies Serving the Blind and Visually Handicapped, 100, 238, 239
National Assembly for Social Policy and Development, see National Assembly of National Voluntary Health and Social Welfare Organizations

National Assembly of National Voluntary Health and Social Welfare Organizations (National Social Welfare Assembly, National Assembly for Social Policy and Development), 94–96, 104 n. 25., 105 n. 28., 119–122, 124 n. 2., 124 n. 12., 125 n. 13., 125 n. 15., 137, 138, 149, 169, 170, 179 n. 16., 179 n. 17., 199, 201 n. 7.; "Voluntary Giving and Tax Policy—Charity is not a Loophole," 121, 124 n. 2.

National Center for Voluntary Action, 43, 122, 184, 185, 201 n. 2.

National Conference of Charities and Corrections, see National Conference on Social Welfare

National Conference of Commissioners on Uniform State Laws, 70, 71

National Conference on Social Welfare, 32

National Council for Homemaker-Home Health Aide Services, 100, 193

National Council of Jewish Women, 55

National Council of Negro Women, 59

National Easter Seal Society for Crippled Children and Adults, 100

National Foundation (March of Dimes), 82, 83

National Foundation v. Fort Worth, 82

National Health Council, 82, 94–96, 100, 104 n. 25.

National Information Bureau, 71, 84, 93, 97–100, 105 n. 28.

National League for Nursing, 100

National Organization of Women (NOW), 59, 60, 65 n. 11.

National Social Report, 188, 189

National Social Welfare Assembly, see National Assembly of National Voluntary Health and Social Welfare Organizations

National Student Volunteer Program, 61

New York Charity Organization Society, 54, 97

New York School of Philanthropy, see New York School of Social Work

New York School of Social Work, 55

O'Connor, John J., 82

Olsen, Mancur, 189, 201 n. 7.

Parens patriae, doctrine of, 70

Parks, Rosa, 226

Participation, maximum feasible, 227; different perceptions of, 227, 228; implications of, 229; expertise and diversity, 230, 231

de Paul, Vincent (Saint), 27

Peace Corps, 61

Perkins Institute for the Blind (Watertown, Mass.) 31

Perlmutter, Felice Davidson, 175, 176, 179 n. 20.

Peterson Commission (Commission on Foundations and Private Philanthropy), see "Foundations, Private Giving and Public Policy"

Philanthropy, definition of, 40

Philanthropy in the 70s: an Anglo-American Discussion (Ditchley Conference), 123, 125 n. 16.

Philanthropy Monthly, 75, 76, 103 n. 3., 103 n. 4., 103 n. 7., 103 n. 10., 103 n. 11.

Pifer, Allan, 41, 48 n. 5., 90–92, 128, 151 n. 1., 153, 165, 178 n. 1., 179 n. 13., 185, 186, 199, 200, 201 n. 4., 253

Poole, Mary, 59, 60, 65 n. 12.

Professional Standards Review Organizations, DHEW Guidelines, 100, 212

"Progress on Family Problems, a Nationwide Study of Clients' and Counselors' Views on Family Agency Services," by Dorothy Fahs Beck and Mary Ann Jones, 190–192, 202 n. 10., 210, 211, 221 n. 5.

Public money and voluntary organizations, 163–176; schizophrenia in regard to, 165; issues raised for organizations, 166; effects on organizations of receipt of, 167; purchase of service, 167, 168; confidentiality and, 168–170; proprietary agencies, 172; planning and, 173, 174.

Public policy, influencing, 127; definition of, 127, 128; philosophical base for, 129, 130; legal base for, 130–132; responsibility of voluntary organizations for, 134; impact of Internal Revenue Code upon, 135–139; proposed amendments to Code, 139–141; grassroots lobbying, 142; status of churches, 142; legislative history of, 143, 144; allowable legislative activity, 145, 146; expertise versus power, 147, 148

Real Estate Settlement Procedures Act of 1975, 78

Reed, David A. (U.S. Senator), 143, 151 n. 9.

Regulation, complexity of, 69; function of, 69, 70; common-law derivation of, 70; at local levels, 71; overkill, 73–79; at state levels, 80, 86, 87; purposes of, 81; uniformity and reciprocity, 83, 84; limitation on fund-raising costs, 84; relationship of religious organizations to, 85; at federal level, 87–92; public and private roles, 79, 80

"[The] Regulatory Challenge to Social Work," Norris E. Class, 69, 70, 103 n. 2.

Retired Senior Volunteer Program (RSVP), 61
Revenue sharing, 34

Sampson, Charles, 69, 103 n. 1.
Schottland, Charles, 57, 58, 65 n. 8.
Scott, Hugh (U. S. Senator), 139
Seasongood v. Commissioner, 136, 137
Self-regulation, 79, 80, 92–100
Service Corps of Retired Executives (SCORE), 61
Sherry, Paul H., 129, 130, 151 n. 2., 151 n. 3.
Shultz, George P., 154, 155, 178 n. 4.
Smith, Constance, "Voluntary Associations, Perspectives on the Literature," 183, 184, 201 n. 1.
Smith, David Horton, 41, 48 n. 4., 49 n. 8., 49 n. 11., 65 n. 1., 65 n. 2., 66 n. 14., 232, 234, 241, 242, 245 n. 9., 245 n. 11., 246 n. 15., 246 n. 16. "Volunteer Administration," 51–53
Social Security, initial legislation, 33; Medicare, 33
Society for Organizing Charitable Relief and Repressing Mendicity, see Charity Organization Society
Solzhenitsyn, Alexander, 208, 209, 221 n. 2.
Stackhouse, Max, 146, 147, 151 n. 12.
Standards of Accounting and Financial Reporting for

Voluntary Health and Welfare Organizations, 95, 206, 207, 218
Steinman, Richard, 186, 194–196, 201 n. 5., 202 n. 11.
Strauss, Ellen Sulzberger, 59
Suhrke, Henry, 75, 76, 103 n. 3., 103 n. 4., 103 n. 5., 103 n. 6., 103 n. 7., 103 n. 10., 103 n. 11., 103 n. 12.
Surrey, Stanley, 107, 108
Symington, James W. (U. S. Congressman), 139

"[The]Tax Climate for Philanthropy" (Hunter), 117, 124 n. 9.
Tax reform, a major threat to voluntarism, 107; tax expenditure theory, 107–112; issues of equity and progressivity, 115–117; conflict in values, 123.
Tax Reform Act of 1969, 73–75, 87, 102, 254
de Tocqueville, Alexis Charles Henri Maurice, 39
Traunstein, Donald M., 186, 194–196, 201 n. 5., 202 n. 11.
"Trustee," 229, 245 n. 6.
Truth in Contributions Act, 76
Truth in Giving Bill, 78
Ture, Norman D., "The Impact of the Minimum Distribution Rule on Foundations," 75, 103, n. 5.

Ullman, Al (U. S. Congressman), 139, 140
"[The] Uniform Supervision of

Trustees for Charitable Purposes Act," 86, 87

U. S. Sanitary Commission, Organization of, in 1861, 32

United Way of America, 95, 100, 103 n. 8., 220, 221 n. 1., 221 n. 11.; gifts to, 112, 113; budgeting processes of, 113, 157–159, 178 n. 6.; UWASIS, 206, 207

Van Deerlin, Lionel (U. S. Congressman) 78, 79

Vista, 61

Voluntarism, at crossroads, 11; at heart of democratic process, 11; capacity to adapt, 12; definition of, 14, 40–42; encompasses vast universe of action, 15; forces impinging on, 12; fragmentation and homogeneity, 225; future of, 225; necessary governmental policies, 247; necessary voluntary objectives, 247, 248; representativeness and diversity, 225; survival of, 247

Voluntary effort, origin and history, 19–38

Voluntary giving, contributions, 46; sources of giving, 44–46; where did the money go? 46–47;

"Voluntary Health and Welfare Agencies in the United States" (Hamlin Report),

47, 49 n. 18., 73, 87, 94, 104 n. 24., 253

Voluntary organizations, classification of, 40–42; criticisms of, 183–186; do they serve the poor? 189–193; essential characteristics of, 186, 187; numbers of, 42, 43; self-help organizations, 194, 195

"Volunteer Administration," David Horton Smith, 51–53

Volunteers, categories of, 51, 52; changing roles of women, 59, 60; numbers of, 43, 44; recruitment, training, and utilization, 53–57; tax issues, 62, 63

"Volunteers: the Untapped Potential" (Study by Canadian Council on Social Development), 63, 66 n. 16.

Weithorn, Stanley F., 115, 116, 120, 121, 124 n. 7.

Wickenden, Elizabeth, 165, 178 n. 10, 178 n. 11. 178 n. 12., 186, 187, 199, 201 n. 6.

Wilder v. Sugarman, 174, 175

Young, Whitney M., Jr., 188

Young Men's Christian Association (YMCA), 32, 158

Young Women's Christian Association (YWCA), 192; of New Castle, Delaware, 137, 138